Petards in the Low Countries

from the Sixteenth to the Eighteenth Centuries

Petards in the Low Countries

from the Sixteenth to the Eighteenth Centuries

By Drs. J.R. Verbeek

The Pike and Shot Society

The Pike and Shot Society
16 Cobbetts Way
Farnham
Surrey
GU9 8TL

Website: www.pikeandshotsociety.org

First edition, published 2014
Copyright © Drs J.R. Verbeek

Printed by Joshua Horgan, 246 Marston Road, Oxford, OX3 0EL

ISBN 978-1-902768-46-5

Weights & Measures
These are taken from contemporary sources. A toise is a French length of measurement equalling 1.949 m. Inch measurements are most probably Rijnland inches where 1 inch = 2.61 cm. Weight of shot is likely to be in Amsterdam pounds (0.494 kg), whilst weight of powder may be in Nuremburg pounds (0.510 kg). However readers should be aware that there is some controversy over the weight of pyrotechnics.

Cover Illustrations
Front: Petard being used to destroy a palisade (detail)
Rear: After the 'failure' of the hell ships, another of Gianibelli's inventions was launched against the floating bridge across the Scheldt at Antwerp: the *Finis Bellis*, or *Fin de la Guerre*. The details of this unwieldy ship are clearly depicted. A mighty ship, specially designed it seems to overwhelm shore batteries and troops partly covered by dikes, this ship was very vulnerable; in fact it was totally unsuitable for an attack on its own against a linear river obstacle (see page 23).

Contents

Introduction

Not surprisingly,entrances form the weakest point of any fortification; hence a lot of ingenuity has beenfocused on the attack and defence of these places. Stout wooden doors, however strongly constructed and strengthened with iron nails and studs, could all be shattered by brute force. The battering-ram was one of the successful siege instruments used: the constant battering destroyed not only the door, but also the nerves and morale of the defenders. Although successful, the operating of the battering-ram incorporated a number of disadvantages. The ram was manually operated, requiring a lot of manpower, who needed protection against all sorts of missiles, incendiaries, boiling oil, quick lime etc. Of course the construction of the battering-ram itself also had to be protected. Hence the battering-ram was unsuitable for surprise attacks.The introduction of gunpowder made it not only possible to blow in doors, but also to do it by surprise. Several countermeasures were possible against the operation of a battering-ram, for instance by restricting the room in front of a gate, a curved entrance, the construction of a barbican, etc. However these measures were insufficient to counter the blast of gunpowder explosions. In fact the only way to prevent this type of attack was to fill in and close off the gateway with earth and wood, as was usually done with secondary gates during sieges. In times of peace (or more precisely non-siege, when surprise attacks could be considered) this practice was not possible, without harming the normal functioning of the town.

When a black powder charge is exploded in the open, most of the blast effect is lost. This can be remedied by stopping the charge with help of wood, stones or earth, but the required speed of surprise attacks prevented this work. To overcome this the petard was developed. The petard was a kind of mortar, or vase-like vessel/container, in which was placed a compressed powder charge. Due to the strong walls of the metal container and the compression, the blast effect of the powder charge was greatly enhanced, when compared with an explosion in the open.The petard was constructed from bronze, iron, tin or even from wood.[1] The powder charge was ignited through a touch hole. In the Netherlands the petard was often described in documents as a'springbus' (Figs. 1-2).

Petards were not only used to destroy the doors of gates, but also walls, heavy chains, palisades and even ships. In due time special petards were designed to cope with these different objects, called wall-petards, gate-petards, chain-petards and palisade-petards.[2]

---

[1] J.D. Pasteur: *Handboek voor de Officieren van het Korps Ingenieurs, Mineurs en Sappeurs*. Volume 2.2nd enlarged and improved edition. Arnhem, 1837, p. 299.

[2] A. Dolleczek: *Geschichte der Österreichischen Artillerie von den frühesten Zeiten bis zur Gegenwart*. Wien, 1887, reprint 2005, p. 193.

Petard Warfare

The petard was invented in France, where in 1575 for the first time a band of Huguenots used a petard to surprise a small castle in Rouerge. Le Chevalier de Ville wrote on this occasion: 'L'usage de petard n'est pas ancient, c'est une invention toute modern, premierement trouvée & mise en oeuvre en France, d'où elle a passé dans les autres pays'.[3] In 1599 the French Royal army of King Henri IV successfully operated a petard against the gates of Cahors, capital city of Quercy. A year later the famous fortress engineer and petardier in service of the King of France,Du Terrail,used the weapon against the town of Bourg. His family name was Louis Combousier Provencal, but had the honorary title of Seigneur du Terrayl, Sieur du Rattier, etc. Vicomte de Ravel, Chevalier de l'ordre & Cornetto blache de Monseigneur le Daulphine, Baron de Moysack etc. In spite of all these honorary titles Du Terrail had to flee to the Low Countries, where he served as officer. After his reconciliation with the French King, he returned to France, but had to flee again when he killed a French nobleman, Masassy, in the presence of the King. Back in the Low Countries he enlisted as a petardier in the service of Archduke Albertus of Austria, then acting Governor of the Spanish Netherlands.

The precise date of introduction of petards in the Dutch army is unknown to us, but the petard as such is mentioned in the 'Instructie ende ordre voor de Meesters van de Vuyr-wercken' of 31st May 1599.[4] The appearance of a petard closely resembled the bronze apothecary's mortar. This resemblance is more than coincidental: the first petards used could well have been apothecary's mortars.

Recommended by the French King on 5th July 1601, the Frenchmen Pierre de Regis and Pierre de Rogine (names also spelled as Pierre Rogiers and Pierre Roquires) were enlisted for the duration of one year as petardiers in the service of the Netherlands Generality, each receiving a monthly pay of 30 guilders. Upon enlisting they were also paid hand holding money to pay off the inn, where they had stayed in expectation of their appointment.[5] On 20th December 1601 the States General increased their monthly pay to 36 guilders.[6] When the short-term contract of Regis and De Rogine expired in 1602, the States General employed another

---

[3] Translation: The use of the petard is not old, it is a recent invention, first invented and used in France and then copied in other countries. M. LeBlond: *l'Artillerie Raisonnée, contenant la description & l'usage des différentes bouches à feu, avec les principaux moyens qu'on a employés pour les perfectionner, La théorie & la pratique des mines & du jet des bombes.* Paris, 1761, p. 245.

[4] Translation: Instructions for the master artificers. In: *Groot Placaet Boek II*, 353. Reference: F.J.G. ten Raa and F. de Bas: *Het Staatse Leger 1568-1795.* Volume II: *Van het vertrek van de Graaf van Leceister tot het sluiten van het Twaalfjarig Bestand (1588-1609).* Breda, 1913, p. 247.

[5] J.J. Dodt van Flensburg: *Archief voor kerkelijke en wereldsche geschiedenissen, inzonderheid Utrecht.* Volume IV, 1846, p. 111: Resoluties der Staten Generaal 1601: resolution, dated 5th July.

[6] van Flensburg, *op. cit.,* Volume IV, p. 111: Resoluties der Staten Generaal 1601: resolution, dated 20th December.

petardier, to operate petards and hand grenades.[7] This was captain Cosse, a Frenchman, who was paid £20, in addition to his captain's pay. Nothing further is known about his predecessors, perhaps they returned to France. Early 17th century petards were a novelty, operated by specialists. It was not uncommon that not only the petards were lost in action, but also the petardiers! Petardiers were so feared and hated that they were sure to be executed if the fell into enemy hands alive.

As mentioned before, there were countermeasures against surprise attacks with petards. On 30th April 1606 the States General ordered Van Dorth to adapt the gates of the cities of Zutphen, Doesburg and Grol in order to prevent petard attacks. A sum of 3,000 guilders was made available for this work. If this budget was insufficient Van Dorth was to close off some minor gates in order to save money.[8] By doing this the eastern approaches (river crossings) to the Netherlands were protected against surprise attacks from the east.

On 14th March 1603 Prince Maurice gave orders to Jean la Roche, a petardier in Utrecht, to prepare 16 petards of different construction, a great number of grenades and some 'secret inventions' for use by his army.[9] The Provincial States of Utrecht were ordered to supply all needs. Jean la Roche was paid a considerable sum of money for his expenses. Around 1605 La Roche was captured by the Spanish and hung together with his ill-fated servants.[10]

On 25th July 1605 the States General wrote a letter to warn the commanders of Breda and Bergen-op-Zoom against the French captain Du Terrail. This captain had served in both cities and had now entered the service of the Archduke. As we have seen Du Terrail was an able petardier and the Archduke was known to be scheming against either Breda or Bergen-op-Zoom, in order to capture one of these key cities by surprise, treason, by use of a petard, or a combination of these means. This warning alerted the commanders who took several precautions.[11]

In 1605 a surprise attack was undertaken against Bergen-op-Zoom. The Spanish actually used a petard in their attempt. On 21st August Du Terrail crossed the flood plain during low tide with his troops and captured the outer stronghold of Beckaf and the redoubt in front of the St. Joannes Gate. Then he directed his attack towards the Watergate, where he destroyed two strong palisades by use of petards. Next he was able to fix another petard against the gate door. However, during transport the gunpowder charge of the petard had become moist and exploded without sufficient force to destroy the strong wooden door. The exploding petards alarmed the garrison and Du Terrail was forced to flee with his troops, crossing back through the nowrising tide. He left 50 dead and 200 wounded

---

[7] ten Raa and de Bas, *op. cit.*, p. 177.

[8] van Flensburg, *op. cit.*, Volume IV, p. 125: Resoluties der Staten Generaal 1606: resolution, dated 30th April.

[9] ten Raa and de Bas, *op. cit.*, p. 247, note 76.

[10] H.H.P. Rijperman: *Resolutiën der Staten-Generaal van 1576 tot 1609*. Volume 13: *1604-1606*. Rijksgeschiedkundige Publicatiën Grote Serie No. 101. 's-Gravenhage, 1957, p. 533.

[11] Rijperman, *op.cit.*, p. 282.

on the battlefield.[12] These losses give an indication of the scope of a petard surprise attack against a strongly defended fortification.

In September 1605 a second petard surprise attack was tried against Bergen-op-Zoom. The alerted garrison and citizens succeeded in organising their defence in time and the attack failed. During this attack three gates were demolished with petards. Hans Laurens succeeded in capturing one of the petards intact. He presented it to the States General, who on 19th September 1605,recognized his extraordinary bravery with a reward of £50.[13]The type of petard used is unknown; it probably went into the State's armoury for further use.

The job of the petardier remained very risky as he must fear not only the blast of his own petard, but also counterattacks by the enemy (Fig. 3). This was the experienceof a petardier in the State's service during a surprise attack against Gelder on 23rd October 1605. The commander of the attack was the Lord of Pressil with 2,000 infantry and 1,000 cavalry. The petardier was to blow in the gates. After fixing his petards to the doors the petardier failed to ignite them. A soldier of the guard detachment detected the unlucky petardier and shot him dead. The surprise attack was then cancelled.[14]

Later on, Breda, the second town on the Archduke's 'shortlist', was also subjected to a petard-attack; like that of Bergen-op-Zoom,it failed. In January 1606, in the neighbourhood of Tongeren, eleven mounted French noblemen were arrested in the presence of Du Terrail. The group carried utensils used for petard-attacks (Fig. 4). Their intended target was unclear: Breda or even Nijmegen were possibilities. As the Spanish army had hung a State's petardier, the Dutch were not lenient toward the captured Frenchmen. Justinus van Nassau, commander of Breda, suggested torturing three or four of the most prominent Frenchmen to find out the whereabouts of Du Terrail and the intended target.[15]Presumably Du Terrail was not captured along with his French companions.

On 14th March 1606 Du Terrail surprised the town of Bredevoort with his petards. The garrison and part of the civilian population took refuge in the castle, which was kept by them. In a quick counter move an army commanded by Prince Hendrick Frederick van Nassau besieged the town. The Spanish garrison lacked both gunpowder and food and had to surrender Bredevoort on 22nd March 1606.[16]

In the same year Du Terrail was ordered to conduct a surprise attack against Sluis. Count Frederic van den Bergh, who was quartered in Brugge and commanded all Royal troops within the province of Flanders, was to support Du Terrail. He provided 1,200 Walloon soldiers for this operation. After crossing an inundated area during the night Du Terrail cautiously approached the fortress of

[12] A.J. van der Aa: *Aardrijkskundig woordenboek der Nederlanden. Tweede Deel*: B. Gorinchem, 1840, p. 307.

[13] Laboranter: *Varia uit het Ordonnantie-boek der Staten-Generaal, 1603-1614*. In: *De Navorscher*, Volume 23, 1873, p. 435.

[14] L.J.E. Keuller: *Geschiedenis en beschrijving van Venloo*. Venloo, 1843, p. 108, 109.

[15]Rijperman: *op. cit.*, p. 533.

[16] J. van den Sande: *De wakende leeu der Nederlanden. Historie vertoonende 't begin ende voortganck der Nederlandsche oorlogen, ende beroerten, tot den jare 1648*. Amsterdam, 1663, p. 112, 113.

Sluis on 7th June 1606. The front rank consisted of 50 elite carbine-armed soldiers commanded by captain Formento. They were closely followed by some 200 pikemen, under command of Ghelinger, De Cluyckenburg (also spelled Crauckenburg) and a captain of an Irish regiment. The main force consisted of 500 men, armed with arquebuses and pikes, and commanded by Claude le Rezoir, sergeant-major in the service of the Count de Bossut. De Chalons, Mestre de camp, commanded the rearguard. Du Terrail ordered his 25 French specialist soldiers and some Irish soldiers in support to swim the wet moat to reach the Eastgate. Because this gate was difficult to approach it was less well guarded than other gates. With help of special instruments the daring attackers succeeded in lowering the wooden drawbridge. The noise of this action alerted the guard detachment, but in the confusion the first gate was blown with a petard. The petard attached to the second gate door blew a narrow hole in the door, just large enough to let pass two soldiers at the time. The action against the first gate was calmly prepared, but the second gate had to be blown as quickly as possible. In the rush the second petard was probably fixed less securely, the consequence of which was that the whole door was not shattered. The strength of the remains of the wooden door prevented the enlarging of the hole with axes etc. and time was running out for the attackers. Formento and his men passed first through the hole, followed by the Irish captain. The 15 strong guard detachment opened fire from a corps de garde (protected guardhouse), instantly killing Formento and Ghelinger. As result the attackers lost courage, fled through the narrow hole and jumped from the bridge into the moat. The fleeing soldiers spread panic and disorder amongst the main force and the rearguard who stood ready to follow up the surprise attack.The attackers lost 400-500 men. In the meantime Count Van den Bergh approached with 2,000 men, but when he saw the disordered troops fleeing the battlefield he concluded that his force was too small to take the town by storm. At this very moment the Sluis garrison sallied and Van den Bergh ordered the retreat. Later the States ordered the construction of a half-moon in front of the gate, which was to prevent future surprise attacks.[17]

The petardier Du Terrail was very lucky to escape death or capture time and again during these ill-fated petard-attacks and seemingly had disappeared. On 10th August 1606, according to the commander of Bergen-op-Zoom, the cunning petardier was spotted in Antwerp.[18] The feared imminent petard-attacksapparently failed to materialise, probably due to the fact that Du Terrail,after a row of failures,had not yet got over the loss of his petards and specialized men. Then at the end of August a letter was intercepted, which revealed the plans of Grobbedonck, military commander of 's-Hertogenbosch, to mount a surprise attack against the town of Tiel. In reaction the States General asked the Raad van State to immediately send a fortification expert to Tiel, in order to adapt the design of the

---

[17] Jaques-Auguste de Thou: *Histoire Universelle de Jaques-Auguste de Thou, avec la suite par Nicilas Rigault; les memoires de la vie de l'auteur. Tome Dixième, 1605-1610.* Livre CXXXVI, Basle, 1762, p. 102, 103.

[18]Rijperman: *op. cit.*, p. 575.

gates to make them petard-proof. Without delay the States General allotted the funds needed for this work.[19] Nowhere is there any link to Du Terrail, but it is highly probable that his service formed part of Grobbendonck's plans.

In 1606Prince Mauritsordered Lord de Chastillon to execute a surprise attack with 2,000 men infantry and cavalry against the town of Venlo. On 30th September 1606, in the evening, the first gate was blown by a petard. At the second gate the petardier tried in vain to ignite his petard and was wounded by the fire from the alarmed guard detachment.[20] Then the guard detachment, reinforced with soldiers of the garrison, drove away the petardiers as well as the assault group supporting them.[21]

In the meantime,due to difficulties with his pay,Du Terrail travelled to Italy, where he offered his services to the Duke of Savoy. He was engaged to undertake a surprise attack at the Swiss town of Geneva. This was no easy task and Du Terrail personally reconnoitred the town's defences. However his moves did not go unnoticed: a warning was send (probably from the Netherlands) to the Geneva authorities, who decided to keep a watchful eye on the petardier. It soon turned out that a soldier of the town garrison informed Du Terrail on the state of defences, guard rota etc. In order to catch Du Terrail in the act the municipal officials of Berne were also informed. A description of Du Terrail's appearance was circulated, his bald head being the most noticeable feature. In the meantime Du Terrail reconnoitred a number of towns that were earmarked as targets. Being an experienced petardier, he succeeded in evading the Swiss countermeasures by staying the night at farms or small villages instead of using inns. He also avoided crowded main roads, but this proved fatal as his horse stumbled on a moor and he drew the attention of a guard detachment, stationed at a mountain-pass. When he was questioned, Du Terrail pretended to be Paulus Constans, a nobleman from Daulphine, on the way to Lorraine to attend court. However someone had seen Du Terrail burning some letters the night before, which was regarded as suspicious. Consequently the would-be Paulus Constans was disarmed and detained and the Geneva authorities were informed. To establish his true identity a Geneva inhabitant, a former soldier, who had served with Du Terrail in the Netherlands, was sent for. This person sat next to Du Terrail, who took fright and, pretending to be ill, went to his room. The former soldier followed him there and admitted his mission to identify Du Terrail. The petardier denied any connections with the Duke of Savoy and predicted certain revenge by the King of Spain and the Archduke if something worse happened to him. He tried to bribe his former soldier with 1,000 Crowns to deliver a letter to the Count of Fuentes. This the soldier refused and instead informed the Swiss authorities of everything. Although Du Terrail was

[19]Rijperman: *op. cit.*, p. 580.
[20]Keuller:*op. cit.*, p. 109.
[21] Jan Waggener: *Vaderlandsche historie, vervattende de geschiedenissen der nu vereenigde Nederlanden inzonderheid die van Holland, van de vroegste tijden af. Negende deel, beginnende in 't jaar 1589; en eindigende met het sluiten van het Twaalfjarig bestand, in 't jaar 1609.* Amsterdam, 192, XXXIV Boek, p. 217.

under Berne jurisdiction, the Geneva government succeeded in his extraction, just in time, as the eloquent Du Terrail had already obtained from his captors the right to write letters and walk freely around the house where he was kept in custody.

When in Geneva Du Terrail denied everything, although pleading guilty probably would have saved him. Evidence against him was mounting: the informer within Geneva confessedand Du Terrail's notes detailing the Geneva fortifications were found. When he was put on the rack Du Terrail revealed his true identity and confessed his intentions. The Duke of Savoy had presented him with a costly jewel and paid him a sum of 700 Ducats for his services. Du Terrail desperately tried to win time, in order to make his influential friends pay, but he was condemned to death by decapitation. On 19th April 1609 he was executed in Geneva at the Place du Molard. Du Terrail went fearlessly and with unbound hands to his execution and presented of his own free will 25 Crowns to Geneva's poor. In vain Lord Desdiguieres had pleaded to convert the death sentence into lifetime imprisonment and in vain Du Terrail's family asked permission to obtain his dead body.Instead Du Terrail was buried at a bastion of the Geneva fortress. The King of France was pleased to hear about Du Terrail's arrest and execution, because of the murder he had committed at the Louvre and his intended surprise attack against Pompelone in Navarre.[22] This is how the life of an unequalled dare-devil nobleman-petardier ended.

In view of the death of the petardier Jean de Crequi dit La Roche, on 30th March 1607 the Dutch States General decided to continue Peter de Regis' appointment as petardier in their service for another year.[23] On 14th April 1607 the States General discussed the request by the Utrecht petardiers David Wynantsz and Adriaen Jansz Dop with regard to a due payment of 1,800 guilders for the preparation of petards, ordered by Prince Maurice. The States General decided first to conduct a precise inventory of all the petards in question, taking note of their weight, material etc. and the estimated price for each type and then decide upon the request.[24] On 19th April, after completingthe inventory, both petardiers were paid the requested 1,800 guilders for the preparation of grenades and petards.[25]

Several other petardiers were mentioned in the States General Resolutions: on 5th March 1614 Lady Prisaille de Verviers, widow of the petardier St. Martin, extraordinary nobleman of the house of His Excellency (Prince Maurice), was paid compensation of 100 guilders on the recommendation of Louise de Coligny (stepmother of Prince Maurice). At the same time Pierre Patrix served the States General as petardier. Living in The Hague was Eduard van Buuren, described as 'petardier di juochi artificiati, grenade et simili', who employed two assistants in

---

[22] E. van Meeteren: *Historie van de oorlogen en geschiedenissen der Nederlanden en derzelver nabuuren, beginnende met den jare 1315, en eindigende met den jare 1611.* Volume 10, Gorinchem, 173, p. 136-149.

[23]van Flensburg, *op. cit.,* Volume V, p. 2: Resolutien der Generale Staten uit de XVII eeuw, meer onmiddellijk betreffende de geschiedenis der beschaving: resolution dated 30thMarch 1607.

[24]van Flensburg:*op. cit.,* Volume V, p. 2: Resolutien der Generale Staten uit de XVII eeuw, meer onmiddellijk betreffende de geschiedenis der beschaving: resolution dated 14th April 1607.

[25]van Flensburg:*op. cit.,* Volume V, p. 2: Resolutien der Generale Staten uit de XVII eeuw, meer onmiddellijk betreffende de geschiedenis der beschaving: resolution dated 19th April 1607.

his service, and was paid a monthly salary of 200 guilders. For his services Van Buuren received a positive certificate, issued by Prince Maurice of Orange.[26]

Several other members of the Crequi dit La Roche family were occupied as petardiers, both in the Netherlands and elsewhere. In 1628 captain petardier Bartholomy Crequi dit La Roche corresponded with the Stateholder in Friesland and in 1647 Swerus de Crequi dit La Roche received a substantial payment for his services to the Doge of Venice. At that time Swerus was between 27 and 30 years of age. Later on he enlisted in the Swedish army and became a major at the Vesterlenske Regiment. In 1647 Bartholomeus Crequi dit La Roche was mentioned as captain petardier. During the English Civil War he operated in England. In 1655 petardier Johan Crequi dit La Roche was in the service of the Portuguese Crown. On 1st November 1672 Stateholder William III ordered N. Crequi dit La Roche to prepare as soon as possible some petards for immediate use. The Crequi dit La Roche family lived in The Hague, occupying a house called 'petardiershuis'. When their petardier business slackenedthe family soon ran out of money to support their expensive lifestyle and they had to move to Monster (a village in South Holland).[27]

In 1641 Daniël de St. André, probably a Frenchman, served as a petardier in the army of Prince Frederik Hendrik. On 2nd January 1642 the Raad van State validated his appointment.[28] In 1651 Bertram de Ricou or Renonceau and Frederik Meineken were employed as petardiers in the service of the States General and in 1660 Johan Elants is mentioned as petardier and engineer of the Generality.[29] Elants earned a monthly pay of 300 guilders. He was also a meritorious cartographer and boasted of being able to draw a map of the German town of Cologne from memory.[30]

When in 1677 the organization of the artillery was laid down the formation included six petardiers, of which only Jan Bincou is mentioned by name; he earned a monthly salary varying between 35 guilders and 92 guilders, 10 pennies (stuivers).The petardiers were supported by 8 drivers (actually called conductors).[31] According to the salary the function of the petardier seems to have been downgraded from the flamboyant nobleman, to a kind of regular engineer or artificer.

Nevertheless petards were still produced by Dutch gun founders: in 1638 the gun founder in the city of Groningen made three mortars and three petards for the Provincial States of Groningen.[32] These petards were certainly cast in bronze. In 1643 the gun founder Coenraet Wegewaert, who operated the States'gun foundryin

---

[26]*Bijdragen voor vaderlandsche geschiedenis een oudheidkunde*, 1918, p. 202.
[27] Communication from Gerard van Eendenburg, researcher of the history of the Crequi dit La Roche family.
[28] F.H.W. Kuypers: *Geschiedenis der Nederlandsche Artillerie van de vroegste tijden tot op heden*. Volume II, p. 251.
[29]Kuypers: *op. cit.*, Volume III, p. 76.
[30]*De Navorscher*, year 40, New Series, volume 23, Nijmegen, 1890, pp 99-100.
[31]Kuypers: *op. cit.*, Volume III, p. 45.
[32] J.Th. van Doesburg: *Letters in Brons*, 1994, p. 66.

The Hague, cast 12 bronze petards ordered by the Generality.[33] Some years later, on 7th June 1646, the Raad van State approved him to cast two small bronze petards, weighing 13 and 15 pounds respectively. In 1672 and 1673 Wegewaert's successor Hermanus van der Nieuwpoort made an unknown number of bronze petards for the Generality.[34]

In 1692 the Generality's siege train included 10 petards in three different sizes according to weight: 30 pounds, 40 pounds and 50 pounds, with a charge of respectively 12, 16 and 20 pounds of black gunpowder.[35] These petards are considerably larger than those described in 1641 by Willem Claesz in his book *Arithmetrische, ende geometrische practijcke der bosschieterye* (issued in Rotterdam), where the largest petard mentioned contained a charge of only 6 pounds. It is clear that the larger petards were less manageable by reason of their weight, but they could deliver a 'greater punch'.

[33] J. MacLean: *Gegevens over de geschutgieters te 's-Gravenhage.* Unpublished manuscript, Amsterdam, s.d. p. 18. Library Institute for Military History, Bureau Documentatie No. 46/3.
[34] MacLean: *op. cit.*
[35] Kuypers: *op. cit.*, Volume III, p. 41.

Description of the Petard and its Use

Willem Claesz's book gives us a detailed description of the petards of his time. According to Claesz the best petards were cast from an alloy of 90% red copper and 10% tin (actually this is the most common alloy of gunmetal or bronze). He describes a large model (A on Fig. 5), which measured 7½ inches at the breech and 5 inches inside. Metal thickness at the breech was to be at least 1½ inches and ½ inch at the muzzle. The diameter at the muzzle was 10 inches. This model weighed 68 pounds and contained a powder charge of 6 pounds.[36]

The smaller model, depicted as B on Fig. 5, was 9 inches tall. Metal thickness was about ½ inch at the muzzle and 1 inch at the breech. The diameter at the muzzle was 7 inches. The weight of the smaller model was 44 pounds; the powder charge was 4 pounds.[37]

In order to have a tight joinbetween the petard and the gate door, or other object that was to be demolished, the petard was mounted on a stout elm board, about 1½ feet wide and 2 feet long.Thickness of the mounting board was 3 inches; the board itself was strengthened with iron bands. The powder charge had to be of the best gunpowder available. The charge was tamped or compressed inside the bore and contained by a wooden plug that was fixed with wooden gussets. The muzzle and wooden plug were usually covered with soot in order to prevent moisture spoiling the powder charge. Sometimes molten wax was used to create a real waterproof cover (as we have seen in the examples of petard operations described above, the petardier sometimes had to cross fields or even a wet moat, so a waterproof cover was a wise precaution).

Diego Ufano, in his description of the petard, reveals another important detail: during filling a wooden rod was placed in the middle of the petard (Fig. 6). The rod was two fingers thick and was placed in such way as to connect with the touchhole. The powdercharge was applied in portions of about ¼ pound weight. The gunpowder was tamped around the rod until the bore of the petard was filled. Next the rod was carefully removed and the resulting hole was filled with fine loose gunpowder that was not tamped or compressed. This ensured a complete and evenignition of the powder charge.[38]

Prior to operation the petard's touchhole was cleaned with the help of a pricker and a slow burning match was attached (but not yet ignited of course!). The petard was fixed using two heavy nails that were driven into the gate door (Figs 7-8). A fork was placed to prevent the petard slipping (Fig. 9). Sometimes a (wet)

---

[36] Willem Claesz: *Arithmetrische, ende geometrische practijcke der bosschieterye.* Rotterdam, 1641, p. 130.

[37]Claesz:*op. cit.*, p. 130.

[38]*Archeleeij: das ist gründlicher Bericht von Beschüss und Gebrauch desselbigen/gestelt und in den Niderländischen Krigen practicirt durch den geübten und erfahrnen Capitän Diego Ufano*, pp. 119, 120.

moat prevented the normalmethod of fixing a petard. In those circumstances the petard could be mounted on a 'trundle' (Figs. 10-12). This cart was constructed from three long wooden planks that were connected and held together with iron bands. The bottom plank had to be of the same width as the wooden mounting board of the petard. Two soldiers wheeled the cart toward the gate door, where the petard itself was fixed with the iron nails.[39]

Kuypers[40] describes a bronze or gunmetal petard that was mounted upon a strong wooden board with an iron hook for easy fixing on a gate door (Fig. 13). Kuypers specifies the following dimensions: the petard was 24 centimetres in length, diameter at the breech was 22 centimetres and at the muzzle 14 centimetres. Metal thickness at the breech was 34 centimetres and 1.7 centimetres at the sides. The petard was fitted with dolphins 8 centimetres in height, 2.5 centimetres wide and 10.5 centimetres thick. These dolphins were for fixing purposes. The wooden mounting board was 55 centimetres long, 47 centimetres wide and 10 centimetres thick. The iron strengthening plates were 8 centimetres wide and 7 millimetres thick. The iron hook protruded 16 centimetres. The wooden mounting board was called a *madrill bert* or *madrier*. Depending on the target and room available the mounting board was either square or rectangular (Figs. 14-17).

In his book *Mauel de l'Artilleur* Théodore Durtubie gives the following description of a petard: the petard was of bell form. Prior to charging the petard was warmed up and the touch-hole was closed with help of a piece of wood or rod. Then the petard was loaded with 2½ pounds of fine gunpowder, mixed with brandy. The muzzle of the petard was sealed with two sheets of grey cartridge paper or felt, onto which a wooden stop was placed. Then a layer of a waterproof mixture, consisting of warm pitch and fine slack of crushed bricks and roof tiles, was put on. Finally the muzzle of the petard was closed with an iron plate with three pointed studs for a firm grip on the bearing board. The loaded petard was placed in an excavation in the bearing board (*madrier*) and fixed with strong iron bands.[41]

In the end of the 18th century the practical use of the petard diminished as result of new developments in fortifications. Durtubie states that in his time petards were only used to blow up gates of smaller towns. When a gate was well guarded or defended with musket fire, the petard attack could only be mounted during night time or when bad weather limited visibility, for instance fog. The storming party had to hide nearby, ready to strike, because obviously the noise of the detonation of the petard would alert the whole garrison: 'les éclats se portent souvent très loin'. Durtubie continues that often an ordinary bomb was sufficient to demolish the gate of smaller towns, which rendered the petard superfluous.[42]

---

[39]Claesz:*op. cit.*, pp. 131-132.

[40] F.H.W. Kuypers: *Verzameling platen betrekking hebbende op de Nederlandsche artillerie in de 16de, 17de en 18de eeuw. 4 platen met verklaring.* Breda, KMA, 1861.

[41] T. Durtubie: *Manuel de l'Artilleur. Cinquième édition.* Paris, l'An Troisième de la République (1791), pp. 240, 241.

[42]Durtubie: *op. cit.* pp. 240-241.

Long after they had lost their operational value and were no longer used, petards were still kept in the inventories of Dutch Republic's arsenals, perhaps considered a curiosity of times gone by. The list of war booty taken by the British on 31st August 1809 during their landings on Walcheren and the South Beveland islands included two petards; thesewere most likely found in the inventory of the Middelburg arsenal.[43]

The Dutch East India Company (VOC) had also petards at its disposal. In 1641 the VOC presented a bronze petard of 135 pounds to 'the emperor of Japan'. Nothing is known about the use of petards by the Japanese. Probably Japanese fortification designs were less vulnerable to petard attacks and as a consequence the petard presented was of limited value to the Japanese. Surely the Japanese were bound to be impressed by the skill and courage required to successfullyoperate a petard.

Finally Le Blond provides us with details regarding an uncommon use of the petard by the Poles: they partly buried the petard and used it as a common mortar to lob stones into a besieged town. The 1659 siege of the then Swedish occupied town of Torn in Prussia is a well-documented example of this practice.[44] In the Netherlands this alternative use is not encountered.

---

[43] Public Record Office, WO 52/194, War Office Bill Books, Board of Ordnance Price Books, fol. 177.
[44] M. Le Blond: *op. cit.*, p. 246.

Naval Petards

On land petards in skilled hands proved a powerful and adaptable weapon; therefore their possibilities in naval warfare were soon considered. At sea there was no need for stealth and surprise as ships often engaged at very close distances. The phase immediately prior to a boarding action promised the most effective results. There were two possible uses, either horizontal (level) or vertical (downwards). However the horizontal use was more suited to damaging or sinking a ship, which was clearly not an advantage for a boarding party. Vertical use could break up the deck of a ship, providing a boarding party with direct access into its hold. The blast also killed or stunned everyone below deck, which was another advantage. On land the petards were carried or wheeled into place; quite obviously this was not possible in naval warfare. A boarding team could not carry a heavy petard and put it into operation amidst the boarding action. It was possible to achieve this goal by dropping or lowering the petard from a protruding yardarm onto the deck of the enemy ship. In theory this could work; in reality there were many disrupting factors, including the erratic operation of a petard and its indiscriminate capacity to sink or damage its own ship as well. Also, even under calm conditions it would be very difficult to move the heavy petard around and place it accurately on the deck of another ship. After placing the petard, it had to be ignited and all friendly personnel had to evacuate the danger zone. This was hardly feasible during a boarding action. Finally naval tactics evolved, placing more weight onto long range artillery fire, instead of bloody boarding actions. So the vertically operated naval petard was probably never used aboard warships.

The horizontally operated naval petard was even more fantastic. The idea was to mount a large petard in front of a small boat and bring the petard into contact with the enemy ship to be destroyed. The small boat had to operate at speed to surprise the presumably larger target. When sails or oars proved not to be suitable to attain the desired speed the designer came up with an incredible idea: rocket propulsion! Lengthwise in the boat two large black powder rockets were mounted to propel it at speed on a ramming course with the target. The petard was ignited by a long fuze, indicating that after igniting the rockets and the delay fuze of the petard no crewmembers stayed aboard. The rudder was fixed. Incredibly this concept bears close resemblance to the 19th century steam propelled lunge torpedo boats, and even more so with the rocket propelled Japanese suicide boats of the Second World War (Figs. 18-19).[45]

---

[45] The incredibility of this concept led the author to undertake a specific check on its source: the original drawing is, since the early 19th century, in the collection of the Netherlands War Department. However the handwriting on the drawing surely dates from the 18th century. These two facts confirm the authenticity of the drawing and the concept depicted on it.

Obviously this 17th century concept was far too advanced for the technologies available at that time. However it was actually tested by the Frenchin 1811 at Villette Bay. The rockets were found to be too weak to power the boat at the required speed to drive the nailinto an enemy ship. It travelled 70 toises. Also the explosive power of the petard was lost, because there was no close attachment to the ship. A torpedo exploding under water was considered more effective, and this was written in 1825![46]

---

[46]*Annales Maritimes and Coloniales* by M. Bajot. Year 1825, 2ndPart, 2nd Volume. Paris 1825, p. 708.

Some Reflections on the Petard's Effectiveness

What about the petards' effectiveness? From descriptions of petard operations in the Low Countries during the second part of the Eighty Years War we learn that the petard was a feared weapon of surprise, evoking a psychological threat far beyond its actual effectiveness. On one hand both friend and foe monitored the movements of active petardiers, and on the other hand any petardier captured alive was hanged. Actions like this hint at a great effectiveness, but also of an aversion against the 'treacherous petardier'. The samefeeling was expressed in the 18th century by a Dutch naval captain who wanted to roast or burn alive every artillerist captured alive, who had fired red hot shot at his ship!

Around the year 1606 the great number of petard attacks is notable. This trend continues during the Thirty Years War (1618-1648), the English Civil War (1639-1651) and the campaigns of King-Stateholder William III. From then petard operations were much less prominent, although there were still petardiers employed. The function of the petardier developed into that of a common engineer or even a honoury title, certainly after the introduction of the rank of 'Chief Petardier' etc. and the actual operation of petards was left to the lower ranks. Also mine warfare became more important. These developments resulted in a loss of the panache associated with the self-opinionated petardiers.

From a technical viewpoint there are two key factors to render a petard attack successful. First a surprise element had to be achieved in order to prevent untimely detection by the guard detachment. Then a sizable body of troops had to be concentrated close to the gate, ready to penetrate the city or fortress by way of the hole blown by the petard. Both factors needed careful planning, organisation, money, perseverance, cold-bloodednessof the petardier and stealth in operating in order to be successful. Usually there were at least two doors to be blown to gain entrance into town. In the case of Bergen-op-Zoom in front of the gate there was a barricade, which had to be blown first. The blowing of barricades, and doors had to be done in succession, which alarmed the whole garrison. That is why the second and third petard had to be mounted in a great hurry, lacking the calmness of the first one. It is noted that the second or third petard usually were less effective than the first one. In 1632 the doors of a Nurnberg gate withstood the violent explosions of three consecutive petards brought into action against it.

The explosion of a petard tended to draw all available soldiers of the garrison like a magnet to defend the endangered gate, leaving other positions undermanned. This situation was exploited by scaling the walls at less defended locations with help of black painted folding ladders that were carried on horseback.

This is how Nurnberg was captured, despite its gate remaining intact.[47] A known failure was caused by the petard flying off: the pressure of the exploding petard did not seriously harm the door, but merely resulted in the petard being thrown off.[48] In order to be successful the petardier had to know about fortifications and the resistance to be expected from wooden doors etc. in order to accommodate the powder charge accordingly. The fuze was lit prior to the attack, after mounting the petard against the door. It was a delay fuze, but the burning time was kept as short as possible, just long enough to get away and effectively restrict possible counter measures by the enemy.

Fortress commanders reacted to this new threat with the better organisation of guard detachments, changes to the construction of the gates and their defences, including closure of less important gates and the institution of 'omrijders' – units or detachments that patrolled the adjacent areas outside the gates walls in order to detect petardiers and hidden troops, ready to perform a surprise attack. A forewarned enemy had ample time to organise their defence, rendering the surprise effect of the petard nil.

Looking at the way the petard is used and its effects, a comparison with the present-day shaped charge is sometimes made, as R.T.W. Kempers does in his book *Antieke vuurwapens*.[49] This is, however, not a valid comparison. In reality there is an enclosed explosive charge that results in a maximum blast/pressure effect. This effect is not reached by mounting the petard against a gate door, because of the improvised character of the fixation. It is the *madrill bert* (mounting board) that closes the gap to the door immediately after the ignition of the powder charge. The strong fixing of the petard to its *madrill bert* causes a short delay resulting in a pressure build-up in the muzzle area of the petard. This pressure is considerably higher than with only a wooden plug. It also partly compensated for an irregular ignition of the gunpowder charge. Of course the construction of the *madrill bert* and iron bands has to be weaker than the walls of the metal petard. The pressure concentrates its effect on the spot of least resistance and pulverizes the wooden mounting boardwith great power.Loss of gas and pressure is limited during this phase. After pulverization of the board the pressure is directed against the gate door, but impacting a greater surface area than just the diameter of the petard muzzle.The fixing of the petard to the door and the supports shoring it up hold the petard in place for just a short time; then a back-blast occurs, shattering the petard and scattering the pieces backwards. However this short period of being held against the door is just long enough to destroy it, even if a lot of the gasses and pressure escape harmlessly.

[47] O. Klopp: *Tilly im dreißigjährigen Kriege. Erster Band, bis zur Zeit des Friedensschlusses von Lübeck 1629*. Stuttgart, 1861, pp. 311, 312.
[48] J. Hiddes Halbertsma: *Hulde aan Gysbert Japiks*. Second Part. Leeuwarden, 1827, p. XLI.
[49] R.T.W. Kempers: *Antieke vuurwapens*. Bussum, 1973, pp. 130 and 132.

The petard was not always destroyed by the effects of the explosion: during a petard operation in Austria the powerful blast blew the petard a distance of 300 metres. Incredibly the petard was found intact and could be used again![50]

The effect of a black powder petard is based on anintentional build-up of pressure, followed by a direction of this pressure from the exploding gunpowder, by successively: a short time delay caused by the mounting board, then a spreading of the blast behind this board and finally a time delay caused by the fixation to the door, with minimal loss of blast effect. The sequence described above takes place within a fraction of a second, but at a much longer duration than a modern explosive charge. The result was a sizeable hole, much larger than attainable with an unmounted petard just placed against a door or a loosely placed explosive charge. Understanding its working principlesone can see the error in comparing the petard with present day hollow or shaped charges. There is no jet of molten metal, issued by the mirror placed on the explosive charge!

Le Blond confirms my theory that the pressure was intentionally spread by the *madrill bert*in order to effect a larger surface area of the door.[51] However, he was unaware of the build-up and direction of the pressure and blast.

---

[50]Dolleczek: *op. cit.*, p. 193.
[51]Le Blond: *op. cit.*, p. 245.

The petard in Sayings, Proverbs etc.

The negative image of the petard and petardier has already been mentioned before (i.e. hanging of any captured petardiers). In Dutch literature this connection is more explicit: in the satirical poems of D. Junius Juvenalis and Aulus Persius Flaccues the petardier is someone who treacherously blows up closed doors of rich mansions, churches and monasteries in order to steal religious and other treasure. Also the noise of an exploding petard is used literally or figuratively to indicate the state of drunkenness, carelessness and sleeping of someone, who is not even awakened by this sound, heralding oncoming troubles.

In England Shakespeare in his masterpiece Hamlet (Act III, Scene IV), framed the sentence 'For tis the sport to have the enginer hoist with his owne petar', stressing the treacherous petardier who is killed by his own petard that goes off prematurely: Polonius perished through his own plots.

In French the word 'pétard' was originally used to describe a loud fart of a horse or cow. The sound of a misfired petard perhaps? Even today some fire crackers are commonly known as chicken's fart.

Conclusion

For a short time the petard was a feared weapon, used in the surprise of cities and fortifications. It was a specialist weapon, requiring 'special people' (the petardiers) and the right circumstances to operate effectively. The effects of the exploding petard were quite impressive and other applications were introduced: petards for use against palisades, chains and even ships (Figs. 20-24).

Defensive measures against this fearsome weapon proved quite easy to devise and as a consequence the petard gradually lost its function. The evolution of fortifications rendered the petard an anomaly, suitable only to blow the gate doors of the smallest villages, a task that could also be performed by ordinary powder charges. As larger fortifications could no longer be surprised by blowing a couple of petards, mining warfare was developed. When exploded, a powerful mine could destroy a complete gate or bastion.

Sadly there are no petards left today in the museum collections of the Low Countries.

Annex
Hell ships against Parma's Floating Bridge, 1585

Petards were used to clear all kind of obstacles, like heavy chains, palisades etc. Several specialised designs were made, often too complicated to be of any use. However, sometimes the object was too large to be destroyed in this way, for instance a heavy floating-bridge. During the siege of Antwerp, in 1585 two specially designed hell ships[52] were used to attack a heavily fortified Spanish bridge. The ships were stowed with gunpowder that was put into a masonry chamber. This chamber was designed to cause a large explosion and by this the destruction of the floating bridge. Although not a petard in the classical sense, the hell ship is included here for its similarity of use and the success they achieved.

On 10th July 1584 the Duke of Parma captured fort Liefkenshoek as the first step of his siege operations against Antwerp. When Gent fell into his hands (19th September 1584), work was started to construct a strong floating bridge, intended to close of the River Scheldt.On 25th February 1585 the bridge was ready to be placed between the sconce Sinte Marie on the Flemish bank and the sconce Philips on the Brabant bank. At these locations strong poles were driven into the river bed. These poles were mutually connected with other poles and covered with stout planks. This construction resulted in a strong bridgehead. Between the Flemish and Brabant bridgeheads an extremely heavy floating bridge was mounted. Both bridgeheads and the floating bridge were provided with guns. To ward off any attacks by fire-ships the bridge was protected by anchored vessels that were mutually connected and mounted heavy skewers. Small rowing boats and patrol vessels guarded both sides of this 'choke' (Figs. 26-27).

The Dutch did little to prevent the construction of Parma's floating bridge, mainly because the commander in chief of the Zeeland fleet Bloys van Treslong did not dare to attack the strong Spanish positions. Consequently he was imprisoned for cowardice and replaced by Admiral Justinus van Nassau. Unlike his predecessor he planned an attack on the floating bridge, for which he chose the weakest point, combining an attack by land and sea forces, focusing at one of the bridgeheads. In this way the Spanish ships and artillery on the opposite bank could not interfere and the bridge mounted artillery would be of little use. This limited Spanish artillery power, while the Dutch fleet could use all of theirs at will. Nassau commenced his attack withthe capture of fort Liefkenshoek on the Flemish bank on 3rd April 1585. This attack was supported by warships: musketeers fired from the crow's nests directly at the Spanish soldiers that defended the parapet. The Spanish

---

[52] The word hell ships is used deliberately to distinguish this kind of ship from the ordinary fire-ships, the latter relied on incendiary power to set their intended target aflame.

artillery was dealt with in the same way: the surprised artillerists could only fire four shots and were unable to reload their cannon. After Liefkenshoek the sconces of St. Antonis-Hoek, Terventen and den Oirt fell into Dutch hands. It was intended that soldiers from Zeeland would follow up along the Flemish Scheldt dyke and press home the attack toward Kalloo. From this point the Spanish floating bridge was to be bombarded by artillery. The high earth profile of the dyke would protect the Dutch against incoming Spanish artillery fire. The land attack was commanded by Count Hohenlohe. The Dutch reached Doel, but were pushed back by Parma's forces, who were ferried in by small boats and immediately started the construction of two new sconces, named De Hoop and St. Antonis. The Dutch forces from Zeeland failed to construct a sconce at Liefkenshoek, and as result they could not withstand the Spanish counterattack. Thus failed an essentially sound plan of Justinus van Nassau, who did not dare to attack the bridge with his warships alone.

Meanwhile in Antwerp the Mantuan engineer Federigo Gianibelli made contact with Filips van Marnix, the mayor who was responsible for the defence of the besieged city. Federigo Gianibelli proposed destroying the Spanish floating bridge with help of an exploding hell ship. Marnix agreed to supply three large ships, named *Orange*, *Gulden Post* and the *Gouden Leeuw*, supported by 60 smaller vessels. These smaller vessels would be connected using chains, ropes and beams to form a large half-moon formation which would drift along the river, sweeping away any obstacles. Gianibelli even thought that the force of the mass of ships itself would be enough to disintegrate and disperse the floating bridge. However, due to the high costs involved in the project, the town council could not provide all the ships promised: only two smaller ships and about ten small vessels were provided. The two larger ships were renamed *Hoop* and *Fortuin*. On orders of Gianibelli the internal construction of the ships was partly removed in order to create space for a strong masonry chamber without windows. The walls of these chambers were 5 feet thick. The inner dimensions were 40 feet long and 3½ feet in width and height. After completion the chambers were filled with a powder charge of 6,000-7,500 pounds, for which Gianibelli used a specially treated (enhanced) powder.[53] The masonry chambers were covered with strong natural stones and even massive gravestones to protect the powder charge from Spanish cannonballs. The powder charge of the *Fortuin* was exploded with help of a wheel-lock mechanism that was activated by a clock; that of the *Hoop* was more conventional with long fuses that were drenched in sulphur.Gianibelli ordered the lightingof a small smouldering fire on top of each of the stone chambers, in order to create the impression of a far less harmful or failing fire ship. For distraction the smaller vessels were equipped to represent real 'fire ships'. To obtain maximum results these 'fire ships' were to be sent in small groups: at 30 minute intervals eight mutually connected vessels were to be set floating down the river in the direction of the floating bridge. Some boats

---

[53] According to some sources Gianibelli had invented a more powerful black powder. Mr. Lenselink, a former curator of the Netherlands Army Museum, stated that carefully grained powder is more likely. Gianibelli maintained an air of secrecy in order to charge more money. Anyhow, the resulting explosion was enormous.

were specially prepared for the destruction of floating obstacles: when these encountered an obstacle a powder charge went off. This would confuse the Spanish forces, who would fire all their cannon at these decoys. Then, by surprise, the hell ships were launched, one at the time (Figs. 28-29).

On the evening of 4th April 1585 Gianibelli's hell ships and decoys were set loose. The Antwerp Admiral Jakob Jakobsen commanded the operation. Against Gianibelli's orders he failed to disperse the loosening of the four groups of small ships, resulting in an unintended concentration that greatly benefitted the Spaniards. Also he let depart both hell ships at the same time, spoiling much of the surprise effect! Soon the *Fortuin* drifted and stranded near the Boerinneschans at Oosterweel. The clockwork mechanism ignited the powder charge right on time, resulting in an enormous, but useless explosion. The small burning vessels got stuck against the floating obstacles that protected the floating bridge and remained there without effect. In the meantime the *Hoop* quietly penetrated the line of obstacles and hit one of the bridge pillars in front of the Kalloo bank. The small smouldering fire on top of the deck seemed quite harmless. At that time a great number of Spanish soldiers, commanded by Marquis de Richebours and Gaspar de Robles, Lord of Billy, had taken up defensive positions on the bridge. Suddenly a large explosion partly destroyed the bridge, killing both high ranking officers and many of the soldiers under their command (Fig. 30).

Mayor Filips van Marnix and Federigo Gianibelli threatened to hang the disobedient Admiral Jakob Jakobson for spoiling the effect of the hell ships. A small rowing vessel was sent to undertake a reconnaissance and record the damage inflicted. Its crew had to signal the presence of a gap in the floating bridge by firing some sky-rockets. At the observation of these sky-rockets the Admiral of the Zeeland fleet would fire a gun signal, starting an overall attack. Although the crew of the reconnoitring vessel was promised a large financial reward for their service, they did not dare approach the bridge, as Spanish troops and boats swarmed the area. Instead they reported that the floating bridge was not damaged at all and no sky-rockets were fired. Thus the Antwerp defence force, lacking concrete information, decided against a sally attack. Nor did the war fleet in Zeeland set sail for action, as an unfavourable wind prevented them moving in the direction of the floating bridge without the risk of grounding in the narrow waters. An attack by foot soldiers was defeated by the Spanish forces south of Doel.

Due to the presumed 'failure' Gianibelli faced the noose. However three days later a courier arrived, sent by Hohenlohe from Liefkenshoek. He brought the news that the floating bridge was indeed partly destroyed. He also reported on the hell ship *Hoop*, which had grounded, burning on the Flemish bank near fort Kalloo. Spanish soldiers had boarded the ship in order to extinguish the fire andto prevent the burning ship beginning todrift againtowards the floating bridge. The Marquis of Rysborg and several other high ranking commanders were close by, giving orders. When the *Hoop* exploded suddenly(the time mechanisminitiated the explosion,having being undetected or left undisturbed during the frantic attemptsto extinguish the fire), killing all aboard and many of the high ranking

Spanish officers. Even Parma himself barely escaped, his page standing beside him being killed. Still dazed by the explosion Parma stood up and drew his sword. Soon Parma realised that there was no attack following up from either from Antwerp or Zeeland. He gave orders for the repair of the floating bridge. The design of the bridge was adapted as a result of this attack: it was constructed with moveable sections that could be opened to let any fire ships pass harmlessly (Fig. 31).

Gianibelli was rehabilitated and started transforming the *Oranje* into a hell ship, loaded with a charge of 4,000 pounds of black powder. A time mechanism, like the one used aboard the *Hoop* was no longer available in Antwerp and apparently could not be built again. So more traditional slow burning matches were to be used. In order to prevent extinguishing attempts 24 beer barrels were mounted all over the ship. These were lined with stones and filled with gunpowder and exploded at irregular intervals, rendering boarding very dangerous. Ten ordinary fire ships would support the *Oranje*. In the end only the ten ordinary fire ships were launched against Parma's floating bridge, without gaining any result. Another invention of Gianibelli was used to destroy the bridge: the *Finis Belli* or *Fin de la Guerre* (see back cover).[54] This was a large ship, armoured against heavy artillery fire and itself mounting heavy guns and four protected towers in which musketeers were stationed. It is possible that this creation was designed to support or follow up the attacks of the hell ships, but it was sent out all alone. This heavy ship did not sail well and ran aground near Oorderen, to be captured by the Spanish. The triumphant Spanish soldiers nicknamed the colossus *Caranjamula*.[55] To this day it is unknown why a second attempt using Gianibelli's hell ships failed to materialise. The effect of the explosion of the *Hoop* had surpassed any expectations and there were many large ships available in the city, like the *Oranje* and *Finis Belli*, which were suitable to conversion into hell ships. For some reason the operation itself, and its coordination with land and/or naval attacks, was considered too difficult to achieve. The floating bridge remained in its place sealing the fate of the besieged town. Antwerp had to capitulate to Parma (Fig. 32).

After the surrender of Antwerp Parma inspected the hell ship *Oranje* in person.[56] Gianibelli went into English service. He designed fortifications and an explosive barrier to block the River Thames. His fame as the designer of the hell ships soon started a life on its own: each time the story was repeated the destructive power was increased. The Spanish especially were frightened by these horror stories. This Spanish fear manifested during the Armada campaign in 1588, when the English sent fire ships against the tight formation of Armada ships. The formation was broken, leaving the ships vulnerable to conventional attacks. The fire ships proved to be of the ordinary type, and not the feared hell ships. For more than a century the hell ship remained just another myth of the Dutch Revolt, but in the 17th century its use was reinvented, when in 1693 Dutch and British hell ships, invented by Willem Meester (1643-1701) were used against the French fortifications

---

[54] Translation: End of the war.
[55] Translation: Scaremonger.
[56] van Meeteren: *op. cit.*, p. 243-251.

of Saint-Malo. Willem Meester even invented 'smoke ships' to cover the hell ships (now called machine ships). In front of Dunkirk the attack of the hell ships failed due to a lack of coordination. Meester was blamed for the failure. It was the end of his promising career as an inventor.[57]

---

[57] H. Pieters: *Uitvinders in Nederland. Vier eeuwen octrooien.* Nationaal Archief, 's-Gravenhage, 2009, p. 16-17. See also: Surirey de Saint-Remy: *Mémoires d' Artillerie. Tome Premier.* La Haye, 1741, p. 370, 371 + plate [hell ship for Saint-Malo and Toulon].

Illustrations

Fig. 1: Several types of petards are represented on this early 17th century German engraving. The middle row (nos. 11-15) shows improvised petards, made from iron hoped powder kegs. The inverted shape of number 6 is intriguing; presumably this peculiar shape was to increase the pressure of the exploding gunpowder. The vent is also unusual on this model. However the inverted conical shape is frequently shown on contemporary engravings. As far as known no real examples of this form have survived. Possibly the drawings are just copied from each other.

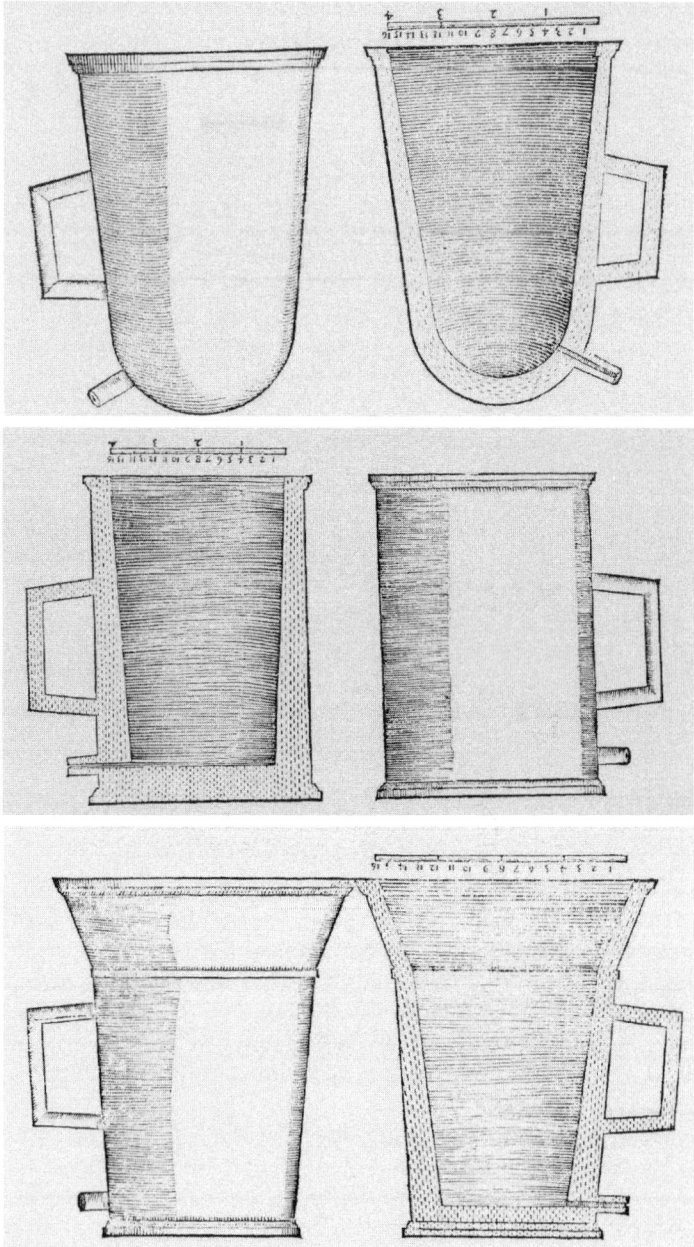

Fig. 2: Three different shapes of petards with a side-mounted vent or touch hole. Source: Christóbal Lechuga, *Tratado de la Artilleria y de Fortificación* (1611).

vn soldat abbat la herse, et tue le petardier

Fig 3: An alerted garrison could prevent a petard attack, as the petardier lacked any cover and had to get close to fix the heavy petard during his attempt to destroy the gate. This picture represents such a situation. The French text says: 'A soldier opens the portcullis and kills the petardier'. This scene comes from the foiled surprise attack on Geneva by the army of Savoy in 1602. It is unclear if a wheeled mantled was used for defence of the gate. Source: François Diodati: *Vraye representation de lescalade enterprise sur Geneve par les Savoyards et sa belee deliverance l'an 1602 XII de Decembre.*

Fig 4: In action the heavy petard and awkward *madril bert* were a difficult load to carry. Mostly this was done by two strong men, as faithfully depicted here. Note the impractical way the first figure depicted is carrying the petard on his own! Lacking in this print are the studs and tools needed to fix the petard to the door. In the foreground stands the petardier with a match and probably a tinder box. Petard attacks were mostly performed at night, complicating the task of the petard crew, who also had to navigate obstacles and even cross moats or swamps with their heavy load.

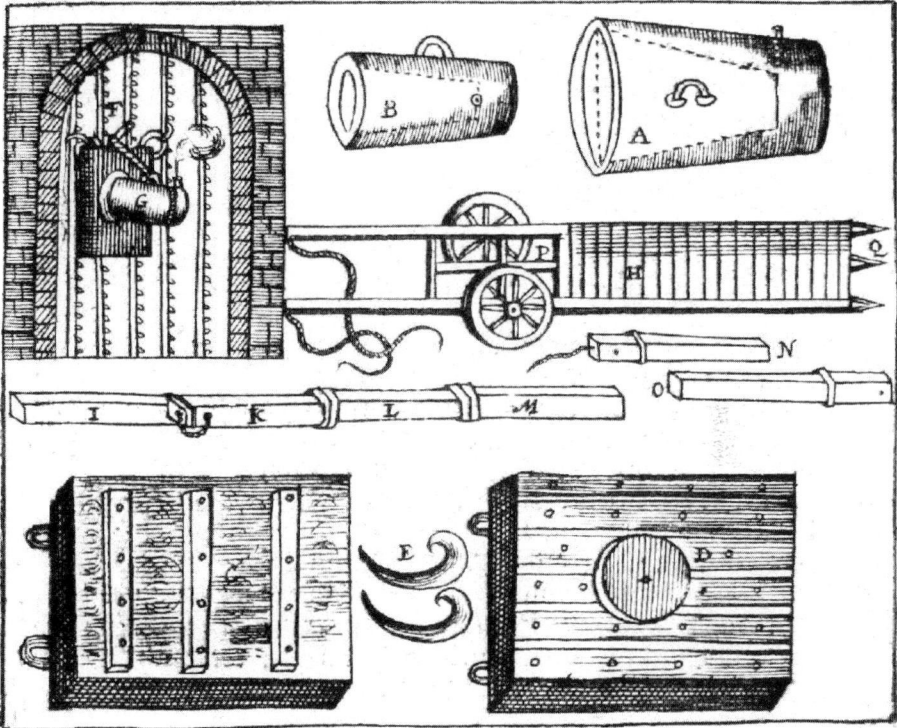

Fig. 5: Petards and storm, or hand cart, described by Willem Claesz in his book *Arithmetrische ende geometrische practijcke der bosschieterije* (Rotterdam, 1641). Clearly for this illustration Claesz largely copied Uffano (see Fig. 6 below). However he corrected the perspective of the fixed petard (G). The petards A and B are of his own invention. K-N are wooden or tin tubes to contain the fuse to light the petard.

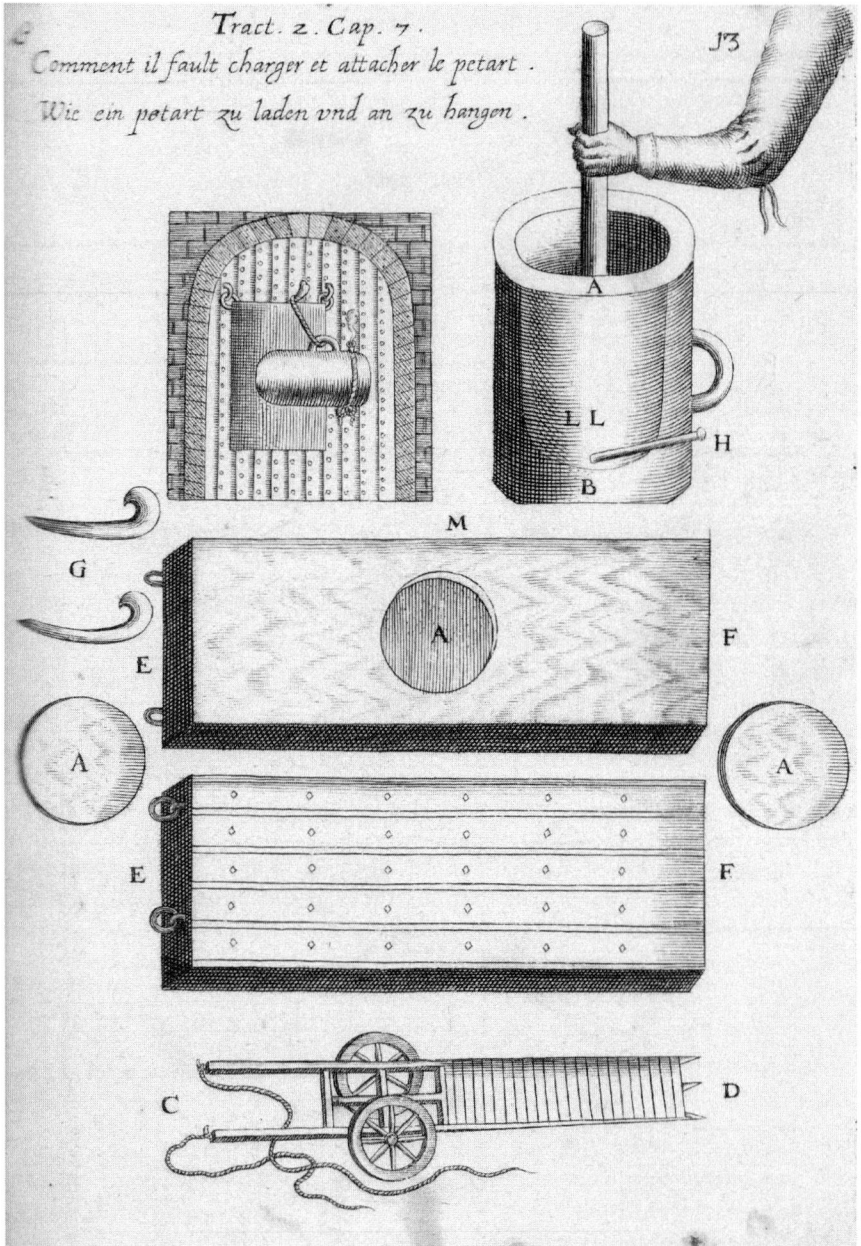

Fig 6: Diego Uffano describes the preparation and use of a petard. In his book he not only depicts the petard and its parts, but also a special cart to drive the petard right up to a gate door. Source: Diego Uffano, *Archeley* (Brüssel, 1613).

Fig. 7: This rather romantic 18th century print depicts the use of the petard in the proper way.

Fig. 8: The various ways to fix the petard against a door or wall are shown in this German engraving. Source: *Andreas Cellarius, Architectura Militaris, 1645. Herstellung und Anbringung von Petarden.*

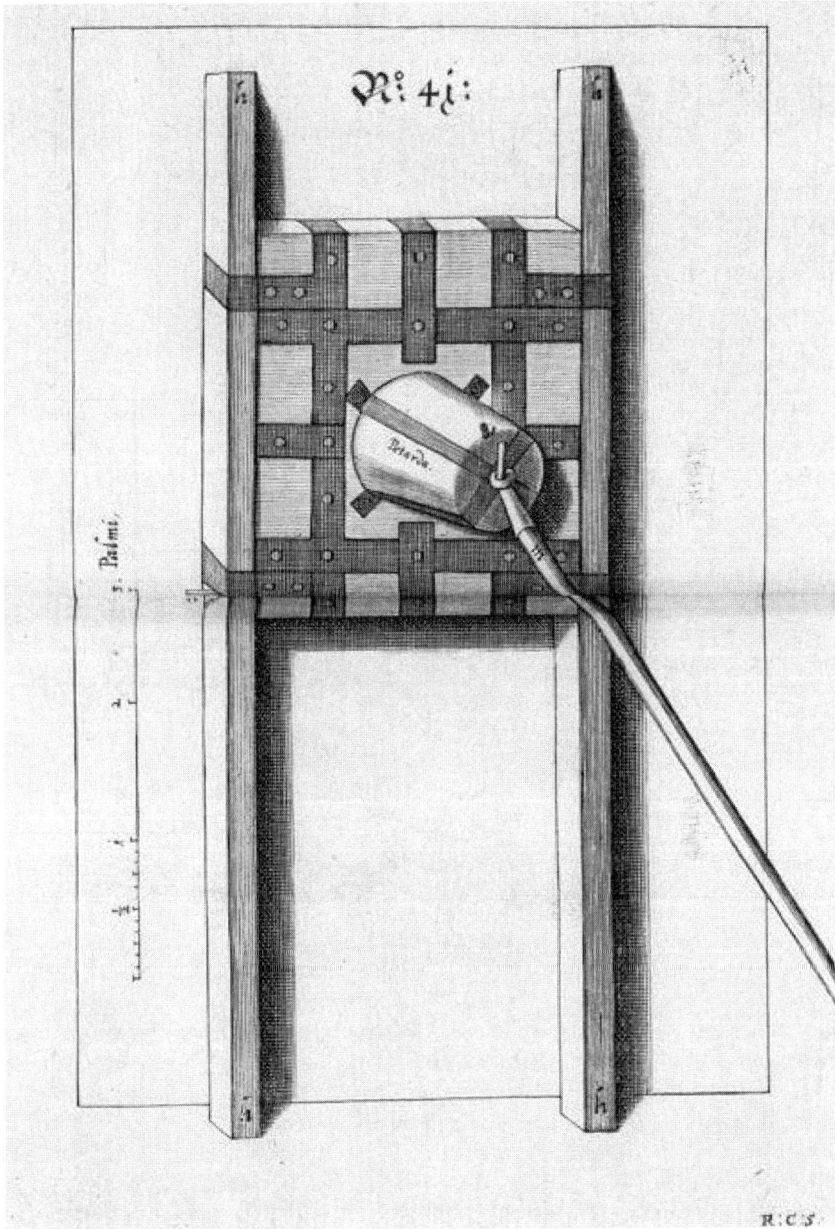

Fig 9: The petard was mounted on a wooden board, called a *madrill bert*, fixed with heavy iron bands. In this picture the petard is kept in place by two wooden legs and a two-pronged fork (gaffel). This way of fixing the petard to the target was stealthier and easier to perform than nailing it to the gate.

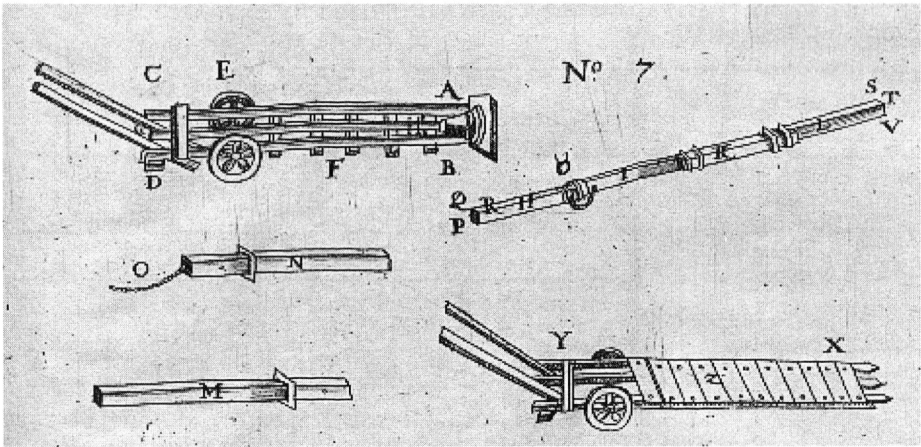

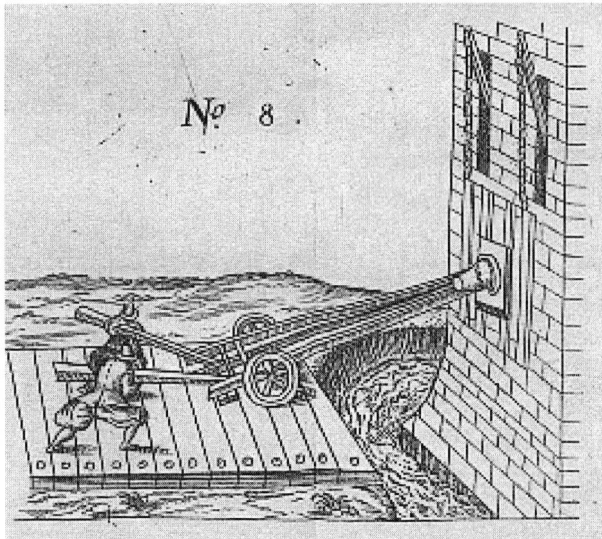

Fig 10: 'Machine' or hand cart of simple construction used to emplace a petard on a distant target. The 'pipes' contain the fuse to activate the petard, as the operation was surely not carried out with a burning fuse. This type of machine was actually in use, as many authors showed their construction. Source: Johann Jacob von Wallhausen: *Corpus Militare. Grundrisse von Festungsbauten, Petarde und Hilfsmitteln zum Anbringen.* 1616.

Fig 11: English petardiers in action. Source: Francis Grose Esq.: *Military Antiquities respecting a history of the English Army from conquest to the present time*, 1812.

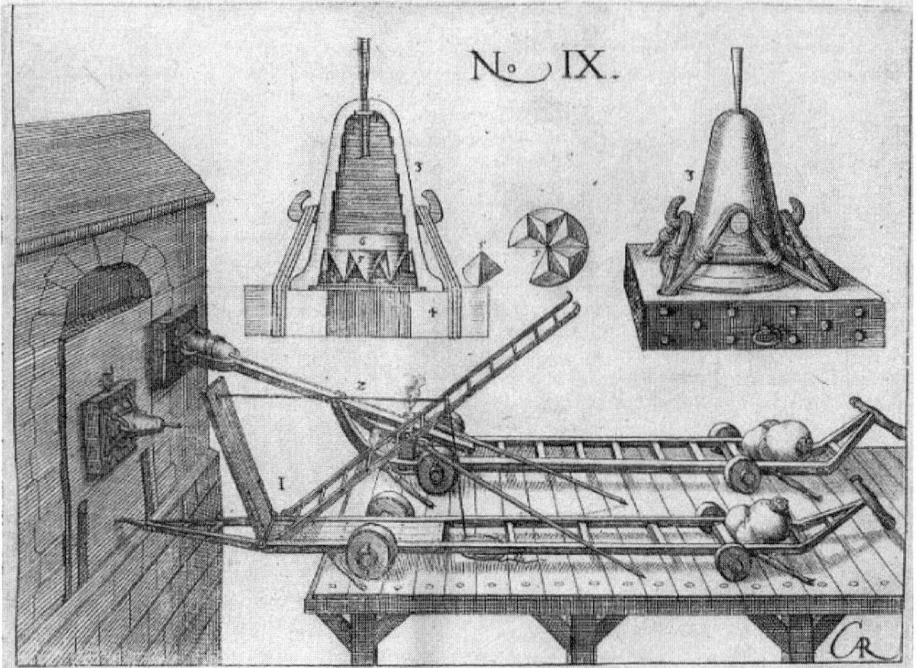

Fig 12: In due time the petard evolved into a more complex weapon, adapted to a variety of circumstances and targets, requiring a 'machine' or pushcart for emplacement. On this German engraving a heavy petard with a dented slug and two elaborate 'machines' is depicted. It seems very likely that most of these kind of 'machines' never went beyond the drawing board stage.

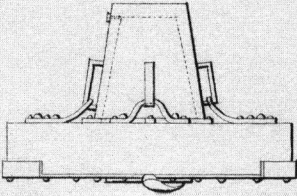

Fig. 16.

Fig. 13: Representation of a petard by Kuypers, a Dutch Artillery officer, who wrote on the history of the Netherlands artillery. Source: F.H.W. Kuypers, *Verzameling platen betrekking hebbende op de Nederlandsche artillerie*, 1861.

Fig. 17.

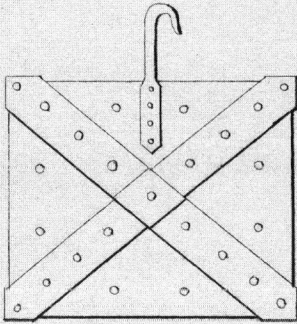

Fig. 18.

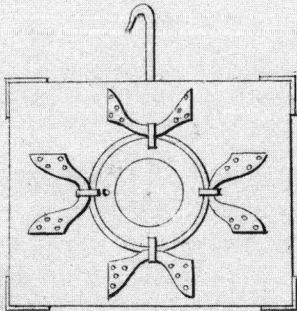

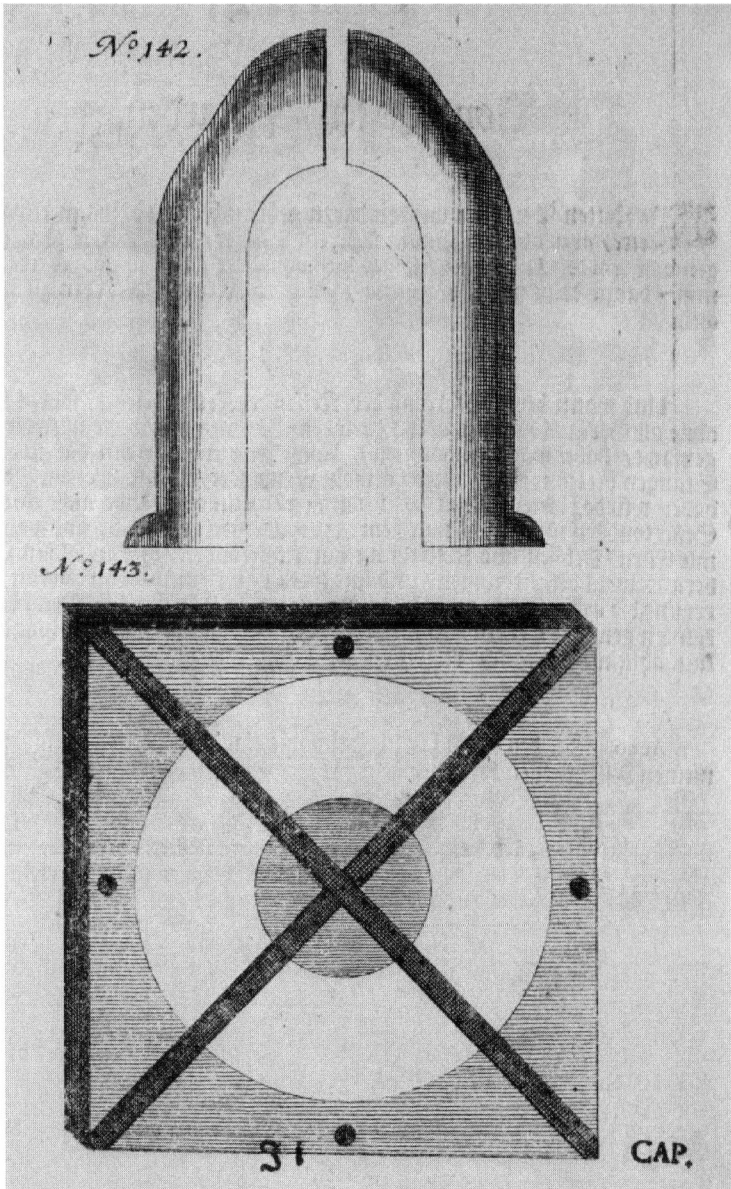

Fig. 14: 6-pounder petard with its square *madrill bert*, as described by Christophe Friedrichs von Geisler, *Neue curieuse und vollkommene Artillerie* (Dresden, 1718). Contrary to most heavy examples, this kind of petard could be carried. The heaviest petards required a 'machine' to bring them in position. Source: Von Geisler, p. 135.

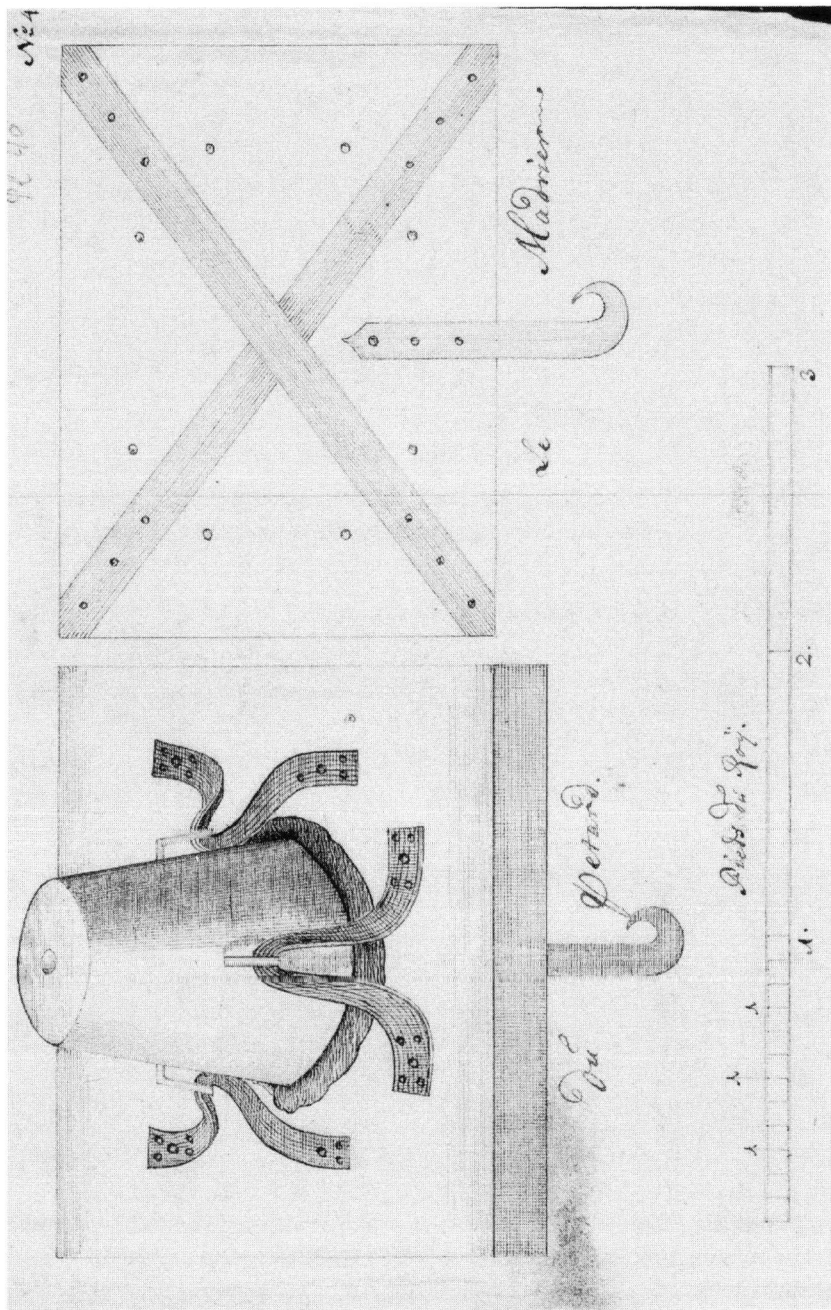

Fig 15: Good representation of a petard and its *madrill bert.*
Source: 18th century drawing, collection of the Netherlands Army Museum.

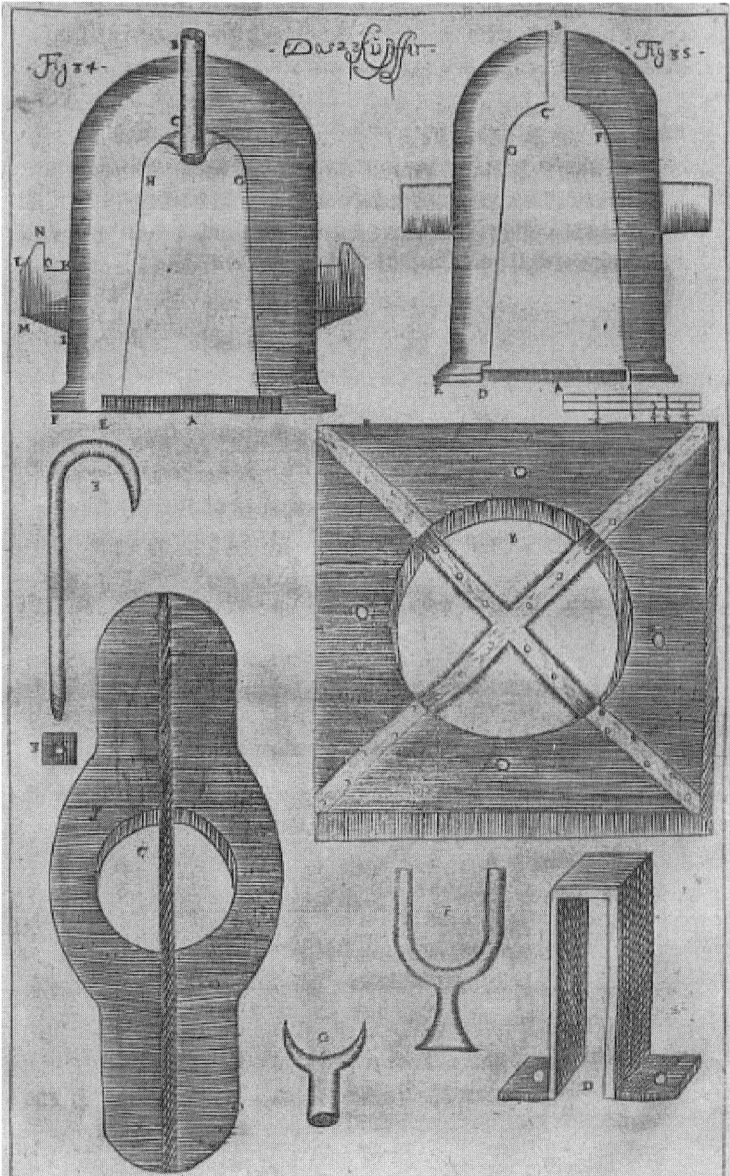

Fig. 16: On this German engraving two types of petards are depicted. What is interesting is that it shows two types of *madrill bert*: a square one (*viereckige madrill bert*) and an oblong one (*längliche madrill bert*). The oblong *madrill bert* was used with a palisade petard to break through palisades. Its oblong shape resulted in a wider horizontal gap than a square *madrill bert* would do.

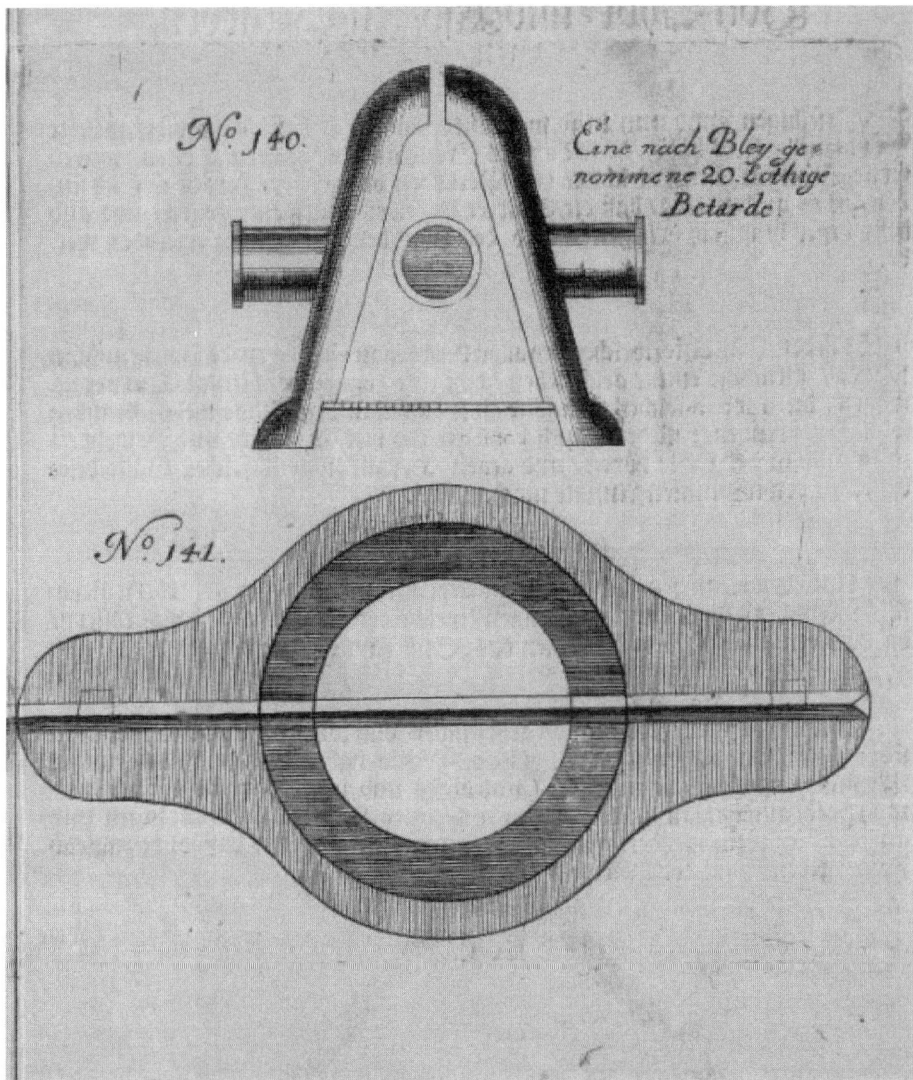

N.º 140.

E. ne nach Bley ge nommene 20. Löthige Betarde

N.º 141.

Fig 17: Palisade petard depicted by Von Geisler. The palisade petard and the gate petard (Thor Petard) were identical, with exception of their *madrill bert*. The choice of which one to use was based on a thorough reconnaissance, preferably made by the petardier himself. This act sometimes raised the suspicions of the garrison, especially when a petard surprise attack was imminent. However without recent intelligence an attack might fail. Source: von Geisler, *op. cit.*, p. 133.

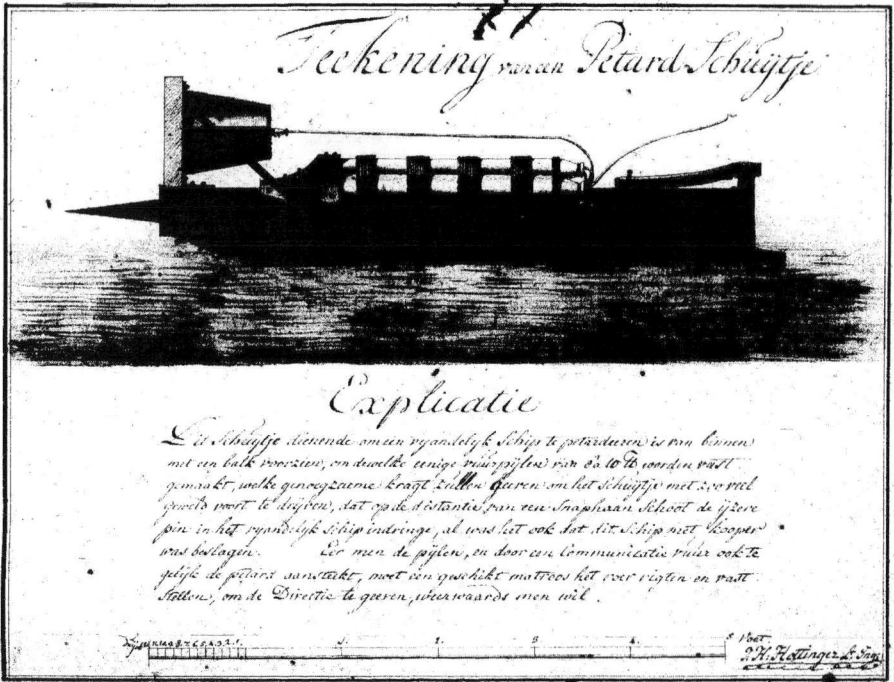

Fig. 18: This Dutch drawing represents the ultimate use of a petard: mounted on a rocket propelled vessel. Predating the WW2 Japanese Shinyo suicide boats by almost two centuries, the idea was to fire the rockets and smash the vessel into an enemy warship. The heavy front-mounted point would fix the vessel in the ship's hull, even if it were copper clad. In the meantime the slow match of the petard was burning, activating the petard with a delay. The size of the petard is enormous and surely would sink or seriously damage any ship targeted. As with the Japanese Shinyo volunteers, the petardier left his vessel directly after lighting the delay fuse, activating the 8 or 10 pound propelling rockets and finally the petard. The operational range of this vessel is stated as 'a pistol shot', which would be 20-30 metres. It was advised to aim the vessel correctly prior to lighting the fuse. Apart from the rocket propulsion this is a feasible concept, aimed at surprising anchored ships. There is no information in the archives linking this invention to a particular individual; the drawing was made by lieutenant engineer Hattinger. It seems to date from the third quarter of the 18th century, at the time of the Fourth Anglo-Dutch War (1780-84). Most originally it formed part of the archives of the Raad van State. Source: Nationaal Archief, collection OMM (drawings of the Ministry of Defence).

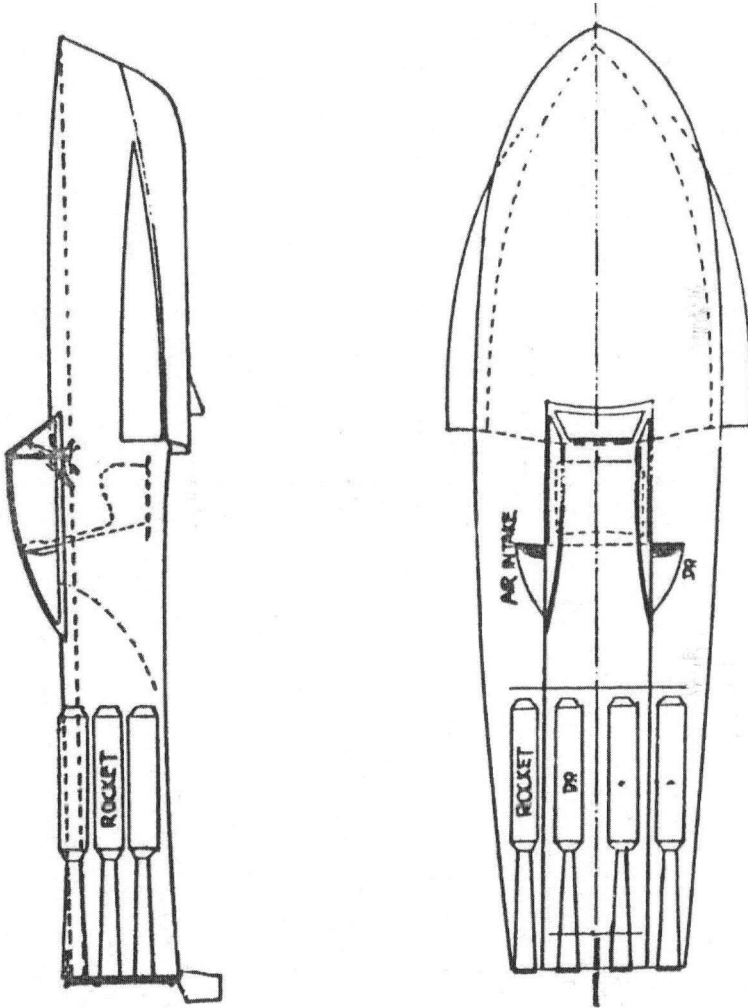

Fig. 19: WW2 Japanese rocket powered suicide boat Shinyo Type 7.

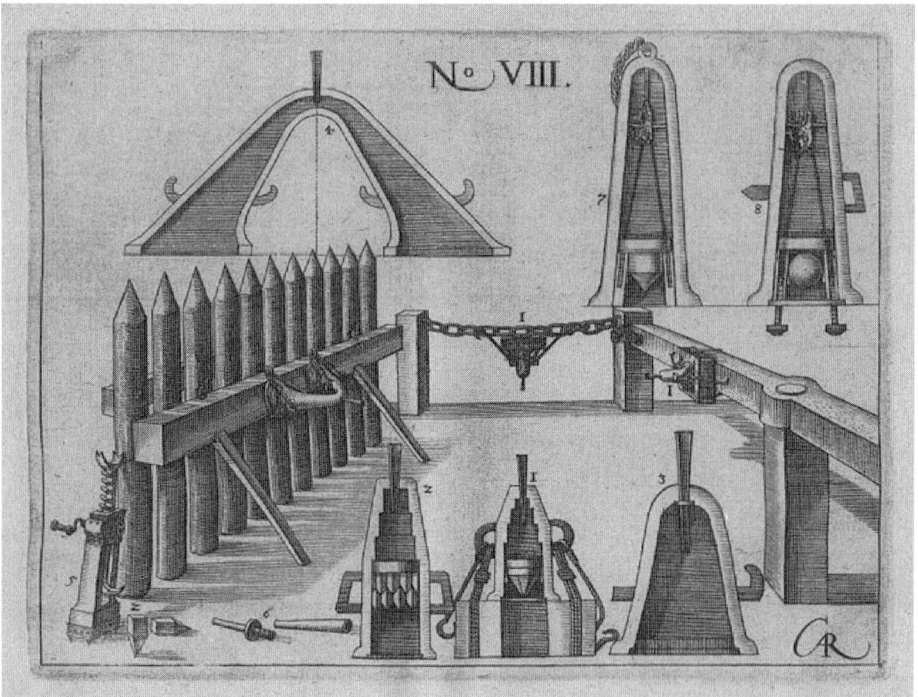

Fig 20: Different types of special petards for breaching palisades, chains etc. Several of these petards have an internal dented or pointed slug for greater effect. Petard Number 4 is a palisade petard; its form is based on the assumption that both 'chambers' will explode at the same time. With the gunpowder technology available and the preparation by hand, this assumption obviously will produce a failure. A succession of two or more petards may result in a better result. Again most of these designs seem to be impractical drawing board projects only. Source: Ulrich von Cranach: *DeliciæCranachianæ*. Hamburg, 1672.

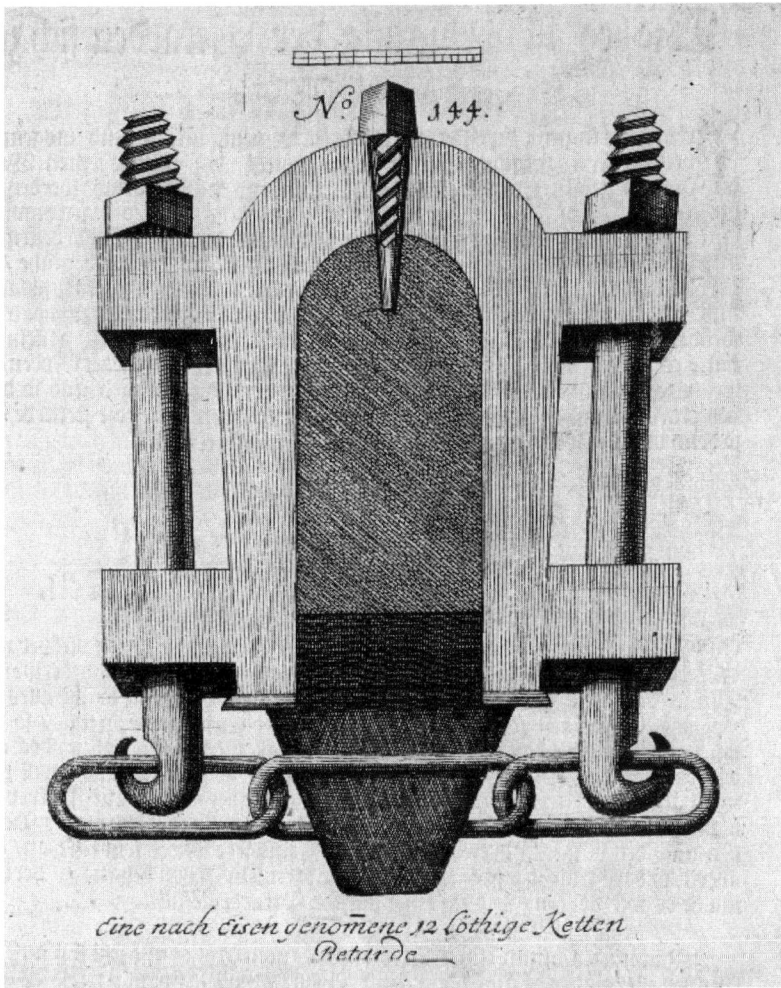

No 144.

eine nach eisen genomene 12 löthige Ketten Retarde

Fig 21: Heavy iron chains were commonly used as very effective obstacles to prevent surprise attacks, vehicle movement or quick entrance. They were used on land to bar roads, on rivers (for example the River Danube), the entrance of harbours (for example the chain near Gillingham, Medway), and even straits (for example the Bosporus). A special chain petard was developed to break through those chain obstacles. To be successful the chain petard had to concentrate its force on one shackle. Several elaborate designs were made, sometimes involving a wedge. As there was no *madril bert* the petard was fixed with hooks to the chain. A chain petard was of a small size, as it could be used only once. When used under wet conditions special care was needed in waterproofing the gunpowder charge. On 3rd July 1689 the chain petard depicted here was made in Hannover after Von Geiser's design. Source: von Geisler: *op. Cit.*, pp. 136, 137.

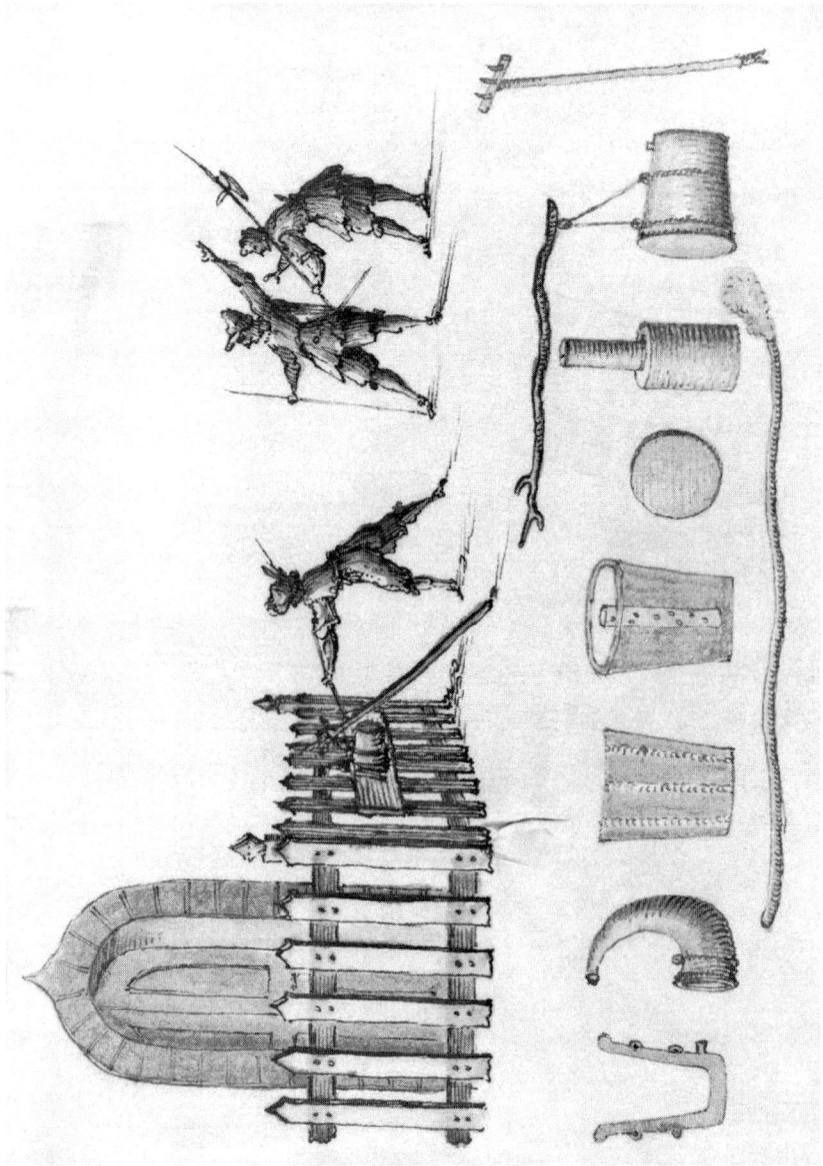

Fig. 22: Petards were frequently used to bring down various obstacles. Often improvised petards were used against lightly constructed obstacles such as ordinary wooden fences, weak stone walls etc.

Fig 23: The petard was not only used to break down gates, palisades, walls etc., but was also used as a kind of directional mine, as shown by illustration 4 in this engraving. Several designs of 'machines' are also present.

Fig. 24: Several solutions were tried to enlarge the blast effect area of the petard in order to create a large opening in, for example, a palisade.This illustration was published in: Surirey de Saint-Remy, *Memoires d' Artillerie, Tome Premier*, La Haye 1741, planche 110. No details are given and this petard was probably included for curiosity reasons.

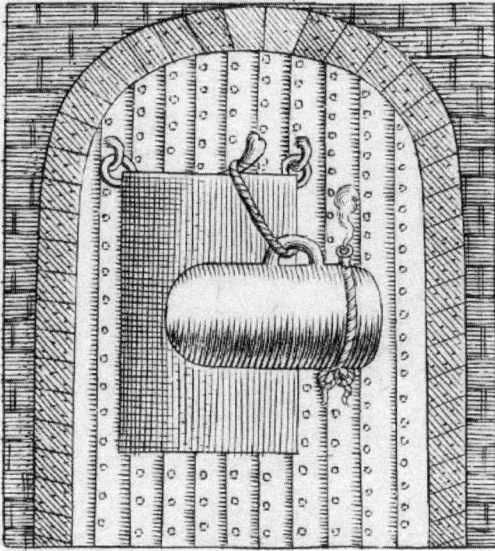

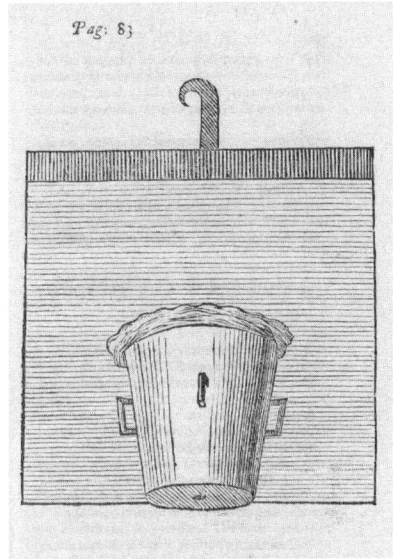

Fig 25: Although the petard was described in various handbooks, many illustrators had never seen a petard and imagination was used to compensate where they lacked details. In particular the fixing of the petard to its *madril bert* and also to the gate was very obscure. This was not for reasons of secrecy, as other parts of the petard were pictured accurately and clearly. As the original drawings were copied by other artists and the petard gradually disappeared from the battlefield this cloak of obscurity remained.

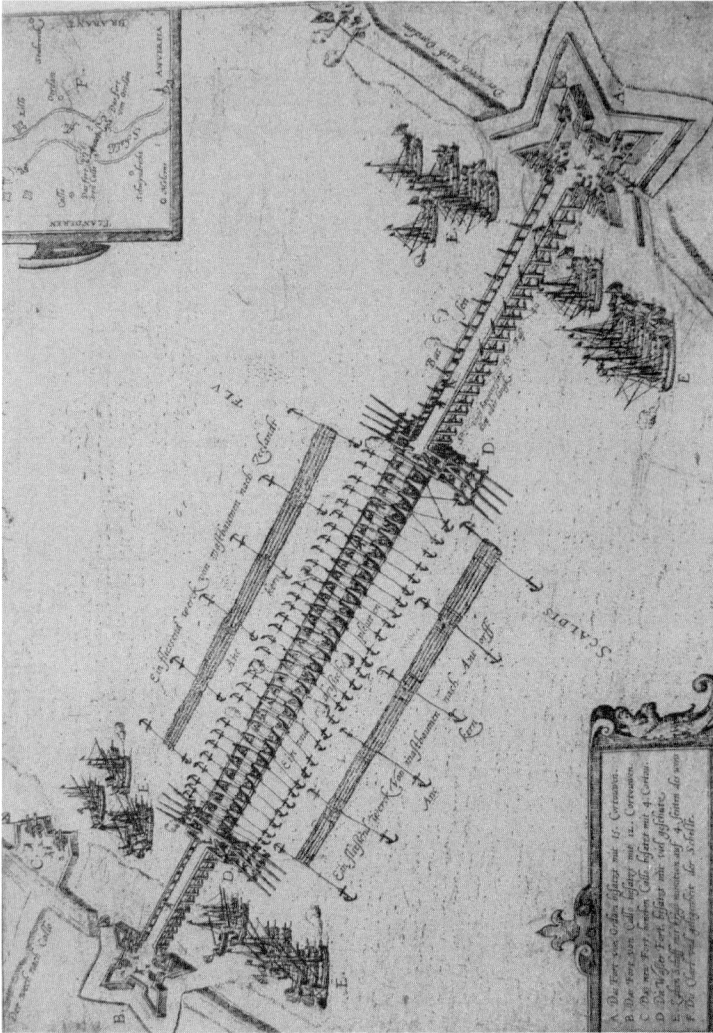

Fig. 26: This illustration provides a realistic representation of Parma's floating bridge that closed the River Scheldt during the siege of Antwerp. It pictures the situation prior to the attack of the hell ships, as the barrier obstacle in front of the bridge has not yet been enhanced. Also, only the ship part, consisting of 31 vessels, is protected by this barrier, the bridgeheads lack this protection. Armament of light anti-personnel (swivel) guns were mounted on the bridgeheads; the heavy guns were emplaced in the fortifications at the ends of the bridge. The fortification on the left side of this picture is fort Kalloo; at the other end is fort Ordam.

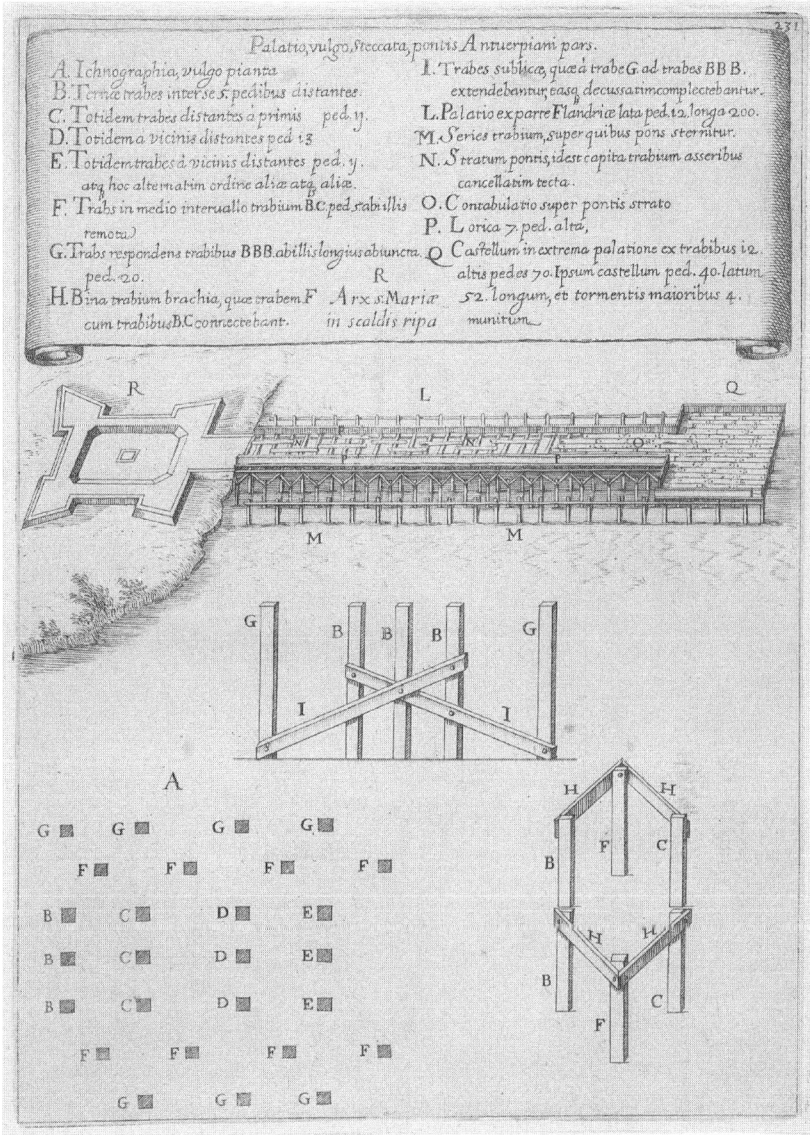

Fig. 27: A realistic illustration of the construction of the bridgeheads, between which the ship bridge was laid. Pictured is fort Kalloo (R), which was armed with 12 Kartouwen (cannon-royal, Spanish 42 pounders) guns. On platform Q another four heavy guns were emplaced: two in the direction of Antwerp and two in the direction of Zeeland. Source: Rijksmuseum, Amsterdam

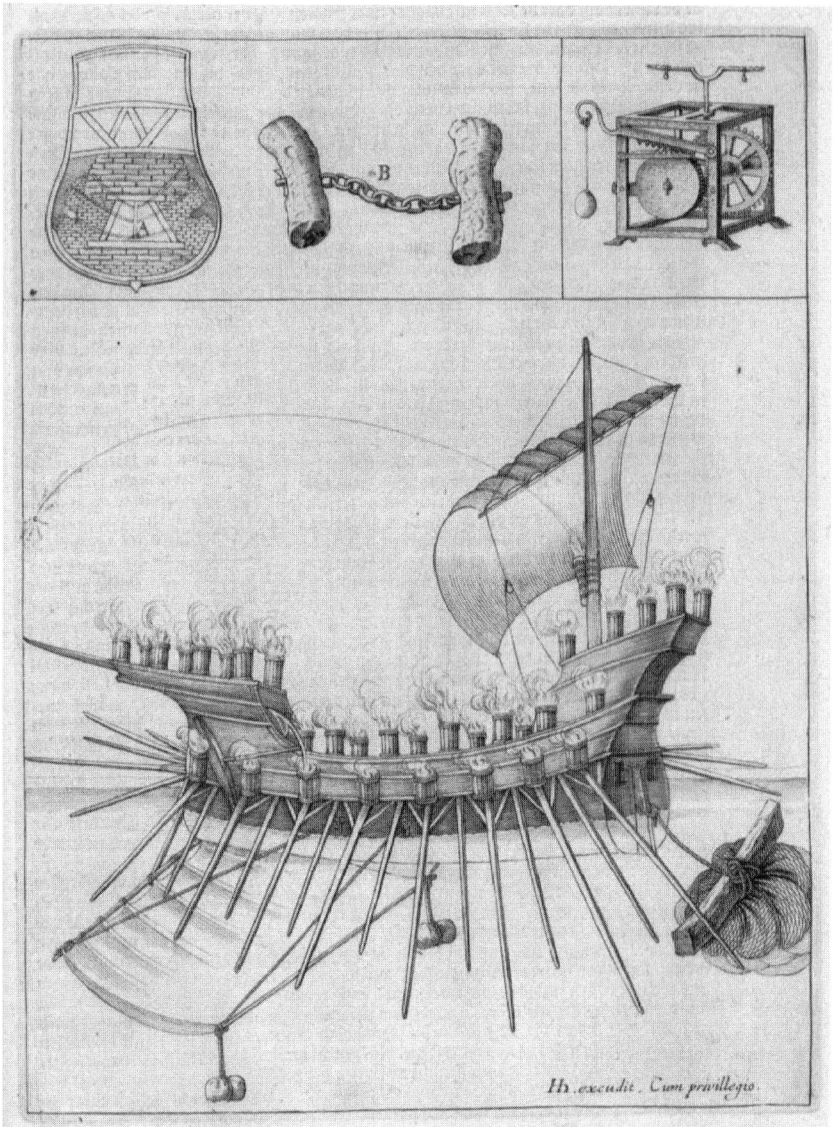

Fig. 28: Illustration of the hell ship designed by the Mantuan engineer Federigo Gianibelli. Above left on the illustration the masonry powder chamber is depicted, including the heavy cover of natural stone. Above right the time clock-mechanism to light the powder charge. The ship is a representation of the *Oranje*, fitted with beer casks filled with powder charges and stakes to prevent the boarding and extinguishing attempts. As the hell ship *Oranje* was captured intact the details are to be considered credible.

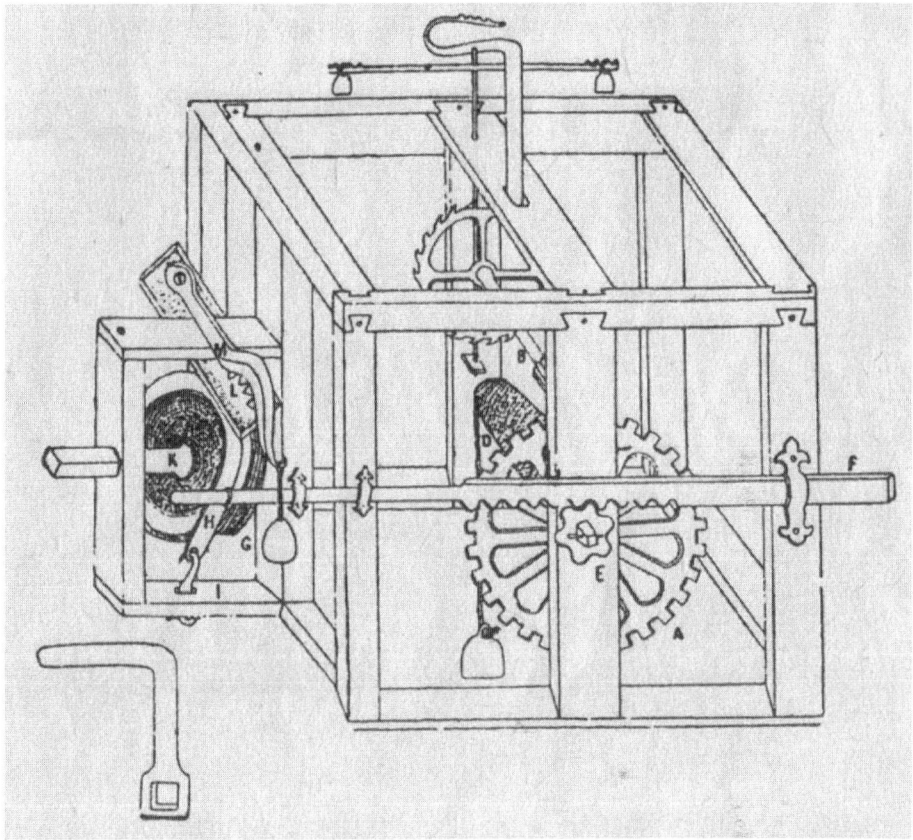

Fig. 29: The time clock-mechanism fitted in the hell ship *Fortuin*. Mounted in the centre is a toothed cog-wheel construction (A and B), connected with a spindle mounting a rope with a weight (D), a pendulum and a kind of a spring-operated wheel lock mechanism (G, H, L), that was activated by bar F, set in motion by toothed wheel E. When the wheel lock was operated a rough surface scraped along a piece of iron (L), creating sparks that would set off the powder charge. The spring (H) was wound with a key, pictured below this part of the machine. Although many details are provided the action of the pendulum, mounted on top of the cage construction, is unclear. It predates the invention of the clock pendulum by Christiaen Huygens for nearly a century! Attention is called to the specially toothed wheel underneath the pendulum, also to be found in clocks of later invention. In all the machine is not a 'time clock' in the common sense, but a rather complex time-delay mechanical fuse. The length of the rope, carrying the weight (D) and the speed of unwinding determined the duration of the delay. This picture differs in many details with the clock shown in the last picture.

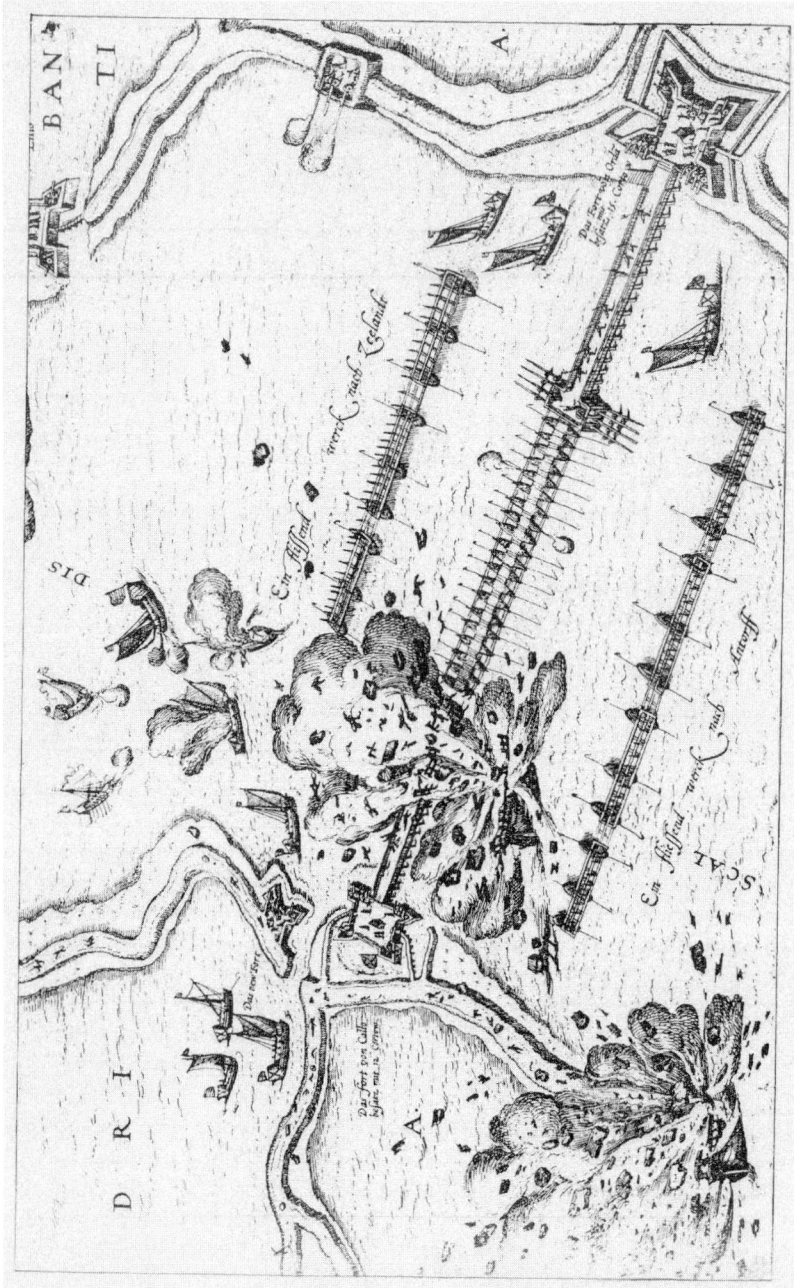

Fig. 30: This picture shows both hell ships – the *Fortuin* and the *Hoop* – exploding respectively on the Flemish bank near Oosterweel and against the Kalloo bridgehead. The location of these ships is more or less accurate, but the drawing gives no clue as to how the *Hoop* had passed through the obstacles.

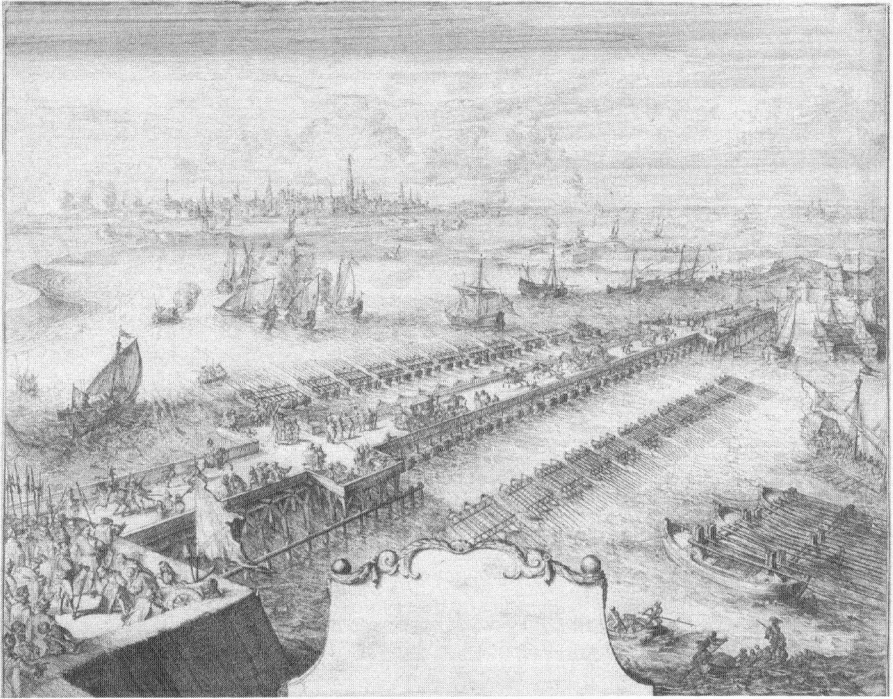

Fig. 31: Parma soon realised that no further attack was to be attempted. He ordered the repair of his floating bridge and the improvement of the protecting barrier defence. Although somewhat 'romantic', this drawing seems to indicate an improved protecting barrier, indicating a period after the hell ship attack. Source: Rijksmuseum, Amsterdam.

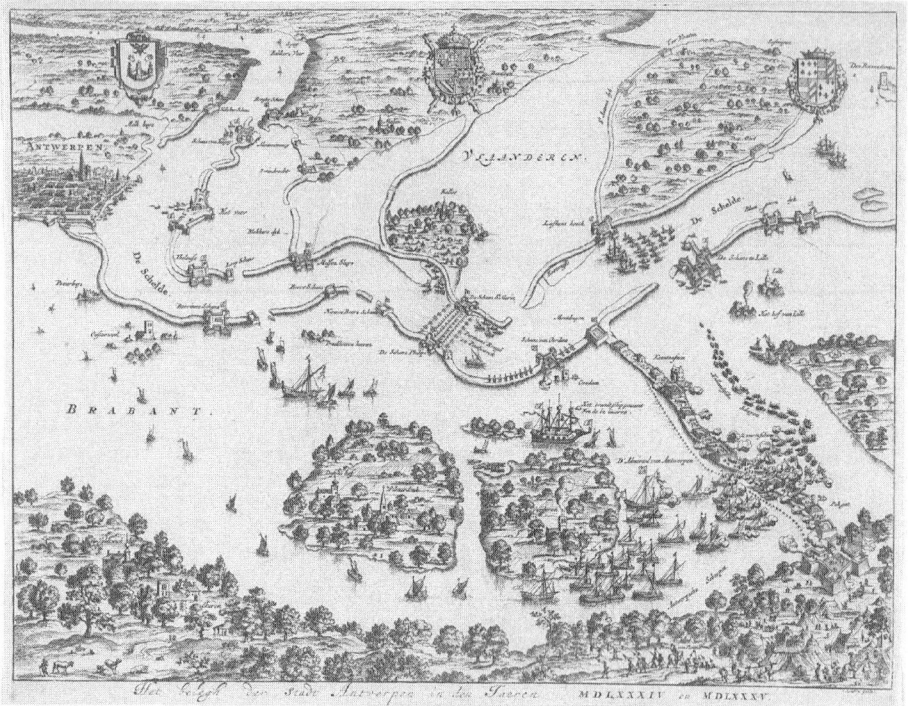

Fig. 32: This bird's eye view map depicts both attacks together: the hell ships (upper right) nearing the floating bridge (centre) with their supporting fire ships following behind and below the unlucky *Finis Bellis* is depicted attacking the 'Pekgat' (bottom right), another closure of the River Scheldt. As both actions were fitted into one map, the relative position is unreliable. However, this was done in order to provide all information about both attacks in a single news pamphlet, which was not unusual for the time.

Select Bibliography

Anon.: *Uittreksel uit de Horen van Schiller betreffende de uitbarsting van een brander te Antwerpen in 1585*. In: Letterbode, vol. 1807, I, p. 130-

Böckler, G.A.: *Manuale Architecturae Militaris*. Vierter Teil. Frankfurt, 1660.

Braun, E.: *Norissimum Fundamentum & Praxis Artilleriæ, oder nach itziger besten Mannier neu vermehrter und gantz Gründlicher Unterricht was diese höchstnützliche Kunst vor Fundamenta habe und erfordere /denn auch/ was vor neue Arthen Canonen/Feuer-Mörser und Haubitzen heutiges Tages im rechten Gebrauch sind /und zu Felde geführet/ auch wie selbige gegossen. Ferner eine vollkommene Beschreibung der Lust-Sachen und Haupt-Feuerwercke*. Danzig, 1682.

Claesz, Willem: *Arithmetische, ende geometrische practijcke der bosschieterye*. Rotterdam, 1641.

Dolleczek, A.: *Geschichte der Österreichischen Artillerie von den frühesten Zeiten bis zur Gegenwart*. Wien, 1887, reprinted 2005.

Durtubie, T.: *Manuel de l'Artilleur*. Cinquième édition. Paris l'An Troisième de la République [1791].

Furttenbach der Ältere, J.: *Büchsenmeisterey-Schul. Darinnen die new angehende Büchsenmeister und Feuerwerker /nicht weniger die Zeugwartten/ in den Fundamenten der Büchsenmeisterey /auch allerhand Feuerwercken underwissen/ und gelehrt werden*. Augsburg, 1643.

Geibig, A.: *Die Macht des Feuers / Might and Fire. Ernstes Feuerwerk des 15.-17. Jahrhunderts im Spiegel seiner sächlichen überlieferung / An object-based survey of serious fireworks of the 15th to the 17th centuries*. Coburg, 2012.

Geisler, Christophe Friedrichs von: *Neue curieuse und vollkommene Artillerie, worinnen Dasjenige /so im 40. Jahren beim 25. Belagerungen/ 24. Eroberungen und 3. Bataillen ausgeübt werden/ in vier nachfolgenden Wissenschaften/ als: Büchsenmeisterey, Ernst-Feuer-Wercken, Petarden und Miniren, angewiesen wird. Nebenst einem kleinen Anhang von Lust-Feuer-Wercken, wie auch Schiff-Brücken/ worüber 2. Halbe Canonen/ nebst einer Bataillon, jedoch geschloßer/ zugleich passiren können, selbst inventiret und vor dem Feind practiciret, mit deutlicher Figuren gantz kurz doch alles aus dem Grunde aufgezeichnet und componiret*. Dresden, 1718.

Godoy, José-A.: *l'Attaque d' une ville par surprise au XVIIe siècle. Pétards et pétardiers*. In: Genava. Revue d'Histoire de l'art et d'archéologie. Genève, 2002 n.s. I, p. 99-154.

Kempers, R.T.W.: *Antieke vuurwapens*. Bussum, 1973

Keuller, L.J.E.: *Geschiedenis en beschrijving van Venloo*. Venloo, 1843

Kuypers, F.H.W.: *Verzameling platen betrekking hebbende op de Nederlandsche artillerie in de 16de, 17de en 18de eeuw. Vier platen met verklaring*. Breda, 1861.

Kuypers, F.H.W.: *Geschiedenis der Nederlandsche Artillerie van de vroegste tijden tot op heden*. Nijmegen, 1873, IV vols, atlas.

Le Blond, M.: *A Treatise of Artillery: or, of the arms and machines used in war since the invention of gunpowder. Being the First Part of Le Blond's Elements of War, written in French. London, 1746.* Museum Restoration Service, Ottawa, 1970 [reprint].

Le Blond, M.: *l'Artillerie Raisonnée, contenant la description & l'usage des différentes bouches à feu, avec les principaux moyens qu'on a employés par les perfectionner, la théorie & la practique des mines & du jet de bombes.* Paris, 1761.

Lechuga, Cristóbal: *Tratado de la Artilleria y de Fortificación. 1611.* Ministerio de Defensa, 1990 [reprint].

Meeteren, E. van: *Historie van de oorlogen en geschiedenissen der Nederlanden, en dezelver naburen, beginnende met den jare 1315, en eindigende met den jare 1611.* Gorinchem, 1751.

Moll, G.: *Over de branders bij 't beleg van Antwerpen in 1585.* In: Letterbode, vol. 1833, II, p. 6-

Pieters, H.: *Uitvinders in Nederland. Vier eeuwen octrooien.* Nationaal Archief, 's-Gravenhage, 2009, p. 16, 17.

Raa, F.J.G. ten; Bas, F. de: *Het Staatsche Leger 1568-1795.* Volume II: *Van het vertrek van den Graaf van Leicester tot het sluiten van het Twaalfjarig Bestand (1588-1609).* Breda, 1913.

Rijperman, H.H.P.: *Resolutiën der Staten-Generaal van 1576 tot 1609.* Volume 13: *1604-1606.* Rijksgeschiedkundige Publicatiën Grote Serie No. 101. 's-Gravenhage, 1957.

Simiecnowicz, Casimir: *The Great Art of Artillery. Fireworks for use in war and peace.* Wakefield, 1971.

Surirey de Saint-Remy: *Mémoires d' Artillerie. Tome Premier.* La Haye, 1741, p. 370, 371 + plate [hell ship for Saint-Malo and Toulon].

Uffano, Diego: *Archeley: das ist gründlicher Bericht von Beschüs und Gebrauch derselbigen /gestelt und in den Niederländischen Krigen practicirt durch deb geübten und erfahrnen Capitän Diego Uffano.* Brüssel, 1613.

van Flensburg, J.J. Dodt: *Archief voor kerkelijke en wereldsche geschiedenissen, inzonderheid Utrecht.* Volumes IV and V. 1846.

Wikipedia Internet document: *Valse hellebranders.* URL: http://nl.wikipedia.org/wiki/Spaanse_Armada, accessed 8th April 2012.

The Pike and Shot Society

Warfare in the Early Modern World 1400 - 1720

We hope you have enjoyed reading this publication and that, if you are not already a member of the *Pike and Shot Society*, you may wish to consider joining.

Founded in 1973, the *Pike and Shot Society* is an international society that promotes interest in the warfare of the early-modern period, a time that saw radical change in the way in which wars were fought world-wide. Its main activity is the publication of its highly respected bi-monthly journal *Arquebusier* as well as specialistbooks, monographs and booklets such as this.

Arquebusier reflects the interests and researches of its members and other military historians. Authors offer material free of charge so the Society keeps its subscription to the minimum. The international nature of the Society means that it has access to unique material, which it publishes for the benefit of members.

In addition to *Arquebusier*, Society members benefit from discounts on a wide range of books and other products of interest. Although based in Great Britain, it is an important aim of the Society to recruit members from around the world. Details of the Society and membership information can be found on our website at:

<u>www.pikeandshotsociety.org</u>

or by writing to:

The Pike and Shot Society,
℅ 16 Cobbetts Way
Farnham
Surrey
GU9 8TL
Great Britain

Publications of the Pike and Shot Society

Uniforms and Colours of the Wars of Louis XIV

- *Flags and Uniforms of the French Infantry under Louis XIV, 1688-1714* by Robert Hall
- *Standards and Uniforms of the French Cavalry under Louis XIV, 1688-1714* by Robert Hall, Giancarlo Boeri & Yves Roumegoux
- *Guidons, Flags and Uniforms of the French Dragoons, Militia, Artillery and Bombardiers under Louis XIV, 1688-1714* by Robert Hall, Yves Roumegoux & Giancarlo Boeri
- *The Army of the Electorate Palatine under Elector Johann Wilhelm 1690-1716* by Claus-Peter Golberg & Robert Hall
- *The Armies of Hesse and the Upper Rhine Circle* by Robert Hall
- *Uniforms and Flags of the Imperial Austrian Army 1683–1720* by Robert Hall and Giancarlo Boeri
- *Spanish Armies in the War of the League of Augsburg, 1688–1697* by Giancarlo Boeri, Josè Luis Mirecki and Josè Palau
- *The Army of the Duke of Savoy 1688 – 1713* by Giancarlo Boeri, with the collaboration of Roberto Vela, Giovanni Cerino Badone and Robert Hall

Renaissance Military Texts Series

- Vol. 1: *Warfare in the Age of Louis XIV*. Three contemporary military tracts from the late 17th and early 18th centuries. Edited by Neil Rennoldson

Other Society Books

- *'An ill jurney for the Englishemen': Elis Gruffydd and the 1523 French Campaign of the Duke of Suffolk*. Transcribed by M. Bryn Davies and edited with a new introduction by Jonathan Davies
- *Elis Gruffydd and the 1544 'Enterprises' of Paris and Boulogne*. Transcribed by M. Bryn Davies and edited with a new introduction by Jonathan Davies.
- *Thomas Audley and the Tudor Art of War* by Jonathan Davies
- *The English Companies of Foot in 1588* by Jonathan Davies
- *The Struggle for Stralsund 1627-1630* by Don McNair
- *La Scherma (The Art of Fencing, 1640)* by Francesco Ferdinando Alfieri. Translated and edited by Caroline Stewart, Phil Marshall & Piermarco Terminiello
- *The Franco-Spanish War: the Sieges of Lleida from 1644 to 1647* by Pierre A. Picouet
- *Waller's Army. The Regiments of Sir William Waller's Southern Association* by Laurence Spring
- *Lostwithiel 1644–The Campaign and Battles* by Stephen Ede-Borrett
- *'Uncharitable Mischief': Barbarity and Excess in the British Civil Wars* by Charles Singleton
- *The Art of Gunnery (1647) together with A Treatise of Artificall Fire-Works (1647) by Nathanael Nye*. Introduction and Transcription by Cliff Mitchell
- *Enniskillen and the Battle of Newtownbutler, 1689* by D.P. Graham
- *Brothers in Arms: The Hamiltons in Ireland, England and France 1610-1719* by D.P. Graham
- *Marlborough Goes to War* by Iain Stanford
- *Eight Banners and Green Flag. The Army of the Manchu Empire and Qing China, 1600-1850* by Michael Fredholm von Essen